The Flowers of Shakespeare

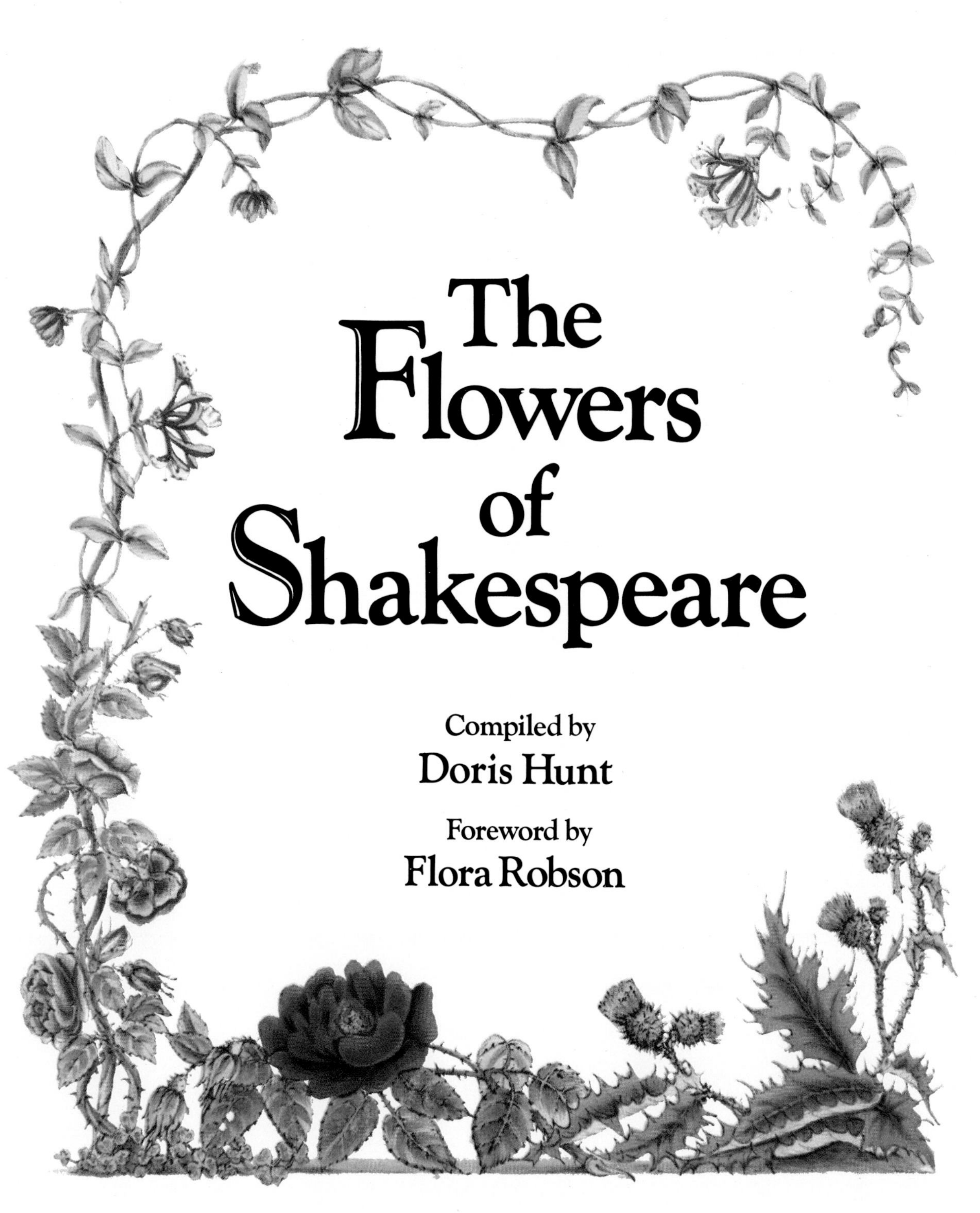

The Flowers of Shakespeare

Compiled by
Doris Hunt

Foreword by
Flora Robson

EXETER, ENGLAND

The publishers would like to thank Mr and Mrs R. E. H. Sturgess, the owners of the original work containing the colour plates, who have made the publication of this book possible.

First published in Great Britain 1980 by
Webb and Bower (Publishers) Limited,
33 Southernhay East, Exeter, Devon EX1 1NS

Distributed by WHS Distributors
(a division of W.H. Smith and Son Limited)
St John's House, East Street, Leicester LE1 6NE

Designed by Peter Wrigley

British Library Cataloguing in Publication Data

Hunt, Doris
The flowers of Shakespeare.
1. Shakespeare, William – Knowledge – Botany
2. Flowers in literature
I. Title
822.3'3 PR3041

ISBN 0-906671-05-1

Typeset in Great Britain by Keyspools Limited, Golborne, Lancs.

Printed and bound in Hong Kong by Mandarin Offset Ltd.

The plates in this book have been reproduced in facsimile and some of the scene references differ from the now generally accepted method of numbering used in the text.

FOREWORD

Flora Robson

The Chaplain of all the Churches of the Isles of Scilly called flowers "the poetry of God". I think that is a perfect and lovely description.

I was named Flora by my Scottish parents so perhaps that is why my imagination is coloured by the beauty of flowers. I still remember my first gift – the top of a large dahlia. I was staying on a country holiday near the Lake District, in a thatched cottage at Wetherall. In the garden below was a gardener who threw up to me the Special Dahlia. That memory of joy goes back over seventy years.

I started voice training when we moved to London. I was five years old and soon I was learning Shakespeare. The first excerpt that I fully understood was from *A Midsummer Night's Dream* – Puck and the fairy:

> And I serve the fairy queen
> To dew her orbs upon the green.
> The cowslips tall her pensioners be . . .
> I must go seek some dewdrops here,
> And hang a pearl in every cowslip's ear.

The Winter's Tale always brings back the joy of flowers and nature:

> When daffodils begin to peer,
> With heigh, the doxy o'er the dale,
> Why then comes in the sweet o' the year,
> For the red blood reigns in the water pale.

There are many such songs of flowers that Shakespeare must have known in his gardens at Stratford on the River Avon.

The Winter's Tale is one of his last plays which he wrote when he had retired to Stratford. This must have given colour to Perdita's flowers.

> Reverend Sirs,
> For you there's rosemary and rue; these keep
> Seeming and savour all the winter long –
> Grace and remembering to you both.
> The fairest flowers of our season
> Are our carnations and streaked gillyvors.

I played Paulina in this play with not a word of poetry in her lines. But she was a highly satisfactory part to play, as honest as she was gormless, like a persistent bad conscience:

> What, sir, I did not well,
> I meant well.

So in that play I *listened* to the flower poetry but had no chance to speak it.

I played Ophelia as a student at the Royal Academy of Dramatic Art and each flower she gave out had a hidden meaning:

> There's Rosemary, that's for remembrance,
> And there is pansies, that's for thoughts,
> Fennel, columbines, rue, daisy, violets.

Writers like Bernard Shaw criticize Shakespeare because he did not write about his own times and because his stories were taken from foreign scripts. But the flowers, they come from Elizabethan England, from the gardens around the Avon, or from the beautiful gardens around London where he worked.

This book will bring them all to mind – the flowers and the poetry.

Flora Robson

INTRODUCTION

All the commentators on Shakespeare are agreed that he was the greatest and most versatile writer the world has yet seen. His knowledge of plants was that which every man may have, but Shakespeare's eyes were always open to the beauties of nature and he did not content himself with merely looking, but tried to find out the inner meaning of the beauty he saw. He had a gift of describing what he saw in a way few others could, not by long descriptions but by a few simple words, a few well chosen epithets.

In his plays, poems and sonnets he names 180 different plants, but he never does so unnecessarily; they all come before us in the most natural way as if that particular flower was the only one that could be named on that occasion.

He was not a botanist and mostly uses the old English words such as daisy, ladies' smock or marigold, except in the cases where the names are derived from the Old French which had superseded some of the native tongue, as we see in eglantine, fleur-de-luce and camomile.

It must be appreciated that London was in those days more rural than urban; there would have been many gardens and Shakespeare could have been familiar with the orchards and knot gardens of his time. Lord Burghley had a noted garden and Gerard (of the *Herball*) was a contemporary.

Just as the architecture of Tudor times was changing from the mediaeval castles and monasteries to the red brick chimneyed houses of peaceful living, so the gardens changed, but perhaps more slowly. The garden still retained surrounding walls for protection, the "alley" walks which were planted with trees and with climbers entwining overhead, and the bowers or arbours which gave a sense of security. These small arbours where lovers met in secret should not be confused with summer houses such as the Princess's pavilion in *Love's Labour's Lost.* The royal pavilions and those belonging to the wealthy were elaborate affairs, for the use of the ladies in summer where they could embroider and enjoy music, and they were also large enough to hold a banquet. There are even descriptions of these built with chimneys and up to three storeys high. Perhaps the rooms indoors were not too pleasant in summer, since so much attention was paid to scented plants. The "curious knot gardens" of formal pattern were bordered with sweet briar, musk rose and honeysuckle, while underfoot were camomile, burnet and thyme.

Shakespeare shows his knowledge of gardening by his many allusions to pruning, grafting and manuring, in addition to weeds, blights and frosts.

> Though other things grow fair against the sun,
> Yet fruits that blossom first will be first ripe.
> *Othello* (ii. 3)

It is interesting to note that while some plays, as *A Midsummer Night's Dream*, were written for a certain time of the year, there are references in others which indicate the season to which the play may be attributed. In *Merry Wives*, with mention of winter's cold, Pistol says, "Take heed, ere summer comes, or cuckoo buds do sing."

In *Hamlet*'s first act "the air bites shrewdly, it is very cold" but after a two-month interval Ophelia's madness must be placed in early summer for although the violets are "all withered", she could pick in abundance fennel, columbines, daisies and pansies.

Autumn is mostly noted by the ripening of fruit, for in Shakespeare's time the many flowers that bloom late in the year had not yet been introduced from other countries such as America. However, it is the spring that Shakespeare mostly enjoys, and so do we.

Oberon's words, familiar to us all, capture the essence of the spring flowers which are mentioned so often in his work, and are the subject of one of the most beautiful paintings in this book.

> I know a bank where the wild thyme blows,
> Where oxlips and the nodding violet grows;
> Quite over-canopied with luscious woodbine,
> With sweet musk roses and with eglantine.
> *A Midsummer Night's Dream* (ii. 1)

Doris Hunt

PLATE 2

eres, most bounteous lady, thy rich leas
Of Wheat, Rye, Barley, Vetches, Oats and Peas;
Thy turfy mountains, where live nibling sheep,
And flat meads thatch'd with stover, them to keep.

Temp

Act. 4th Scene 1st

BARLEY *Hordeum vulgare*

Barley, in plate 2 the spikelet with the long glumes, is the cereal used to this day for making beer, and it must have been so for a very long time for the name comes not from the Latin word but means merely "beer-plant".

> Can sodden water,
> A drench for surrein'd jades, their barley broth,
> Decot their cold blood to such valiant heart?
> *Henry V* (iii. 5)

The food of English soldiers in *Henry V* of which the French Constable spoke so contemptuously was undoubtedly beer, according to Ellacombe who quotes Gerard: "strangers would not know it for it is not everywhere made." Perhaps "broth" is a strange word to describe beer. There is an old-fashioned dish which might come nearer, the "furmity" described by Thomas Hardy in *The Mayor of Casterbridge*, "a mixture of corn in the grain, milk, raisins, currants and what not" which was generously laced in this case with rum.

BINDWEED *Calystegia sepium*

Convolvulus, woodbine or bindweed is a deciduous climber with striking trumpet-shaped flowers, white but sometimes touched with pink. When found in the garden twisting round a valued plant it is looked upon as a pernicious weed, yet if allowed to trail over a leafy hedge it becomes very decorative. The flowers only last a day and often close too soon for the hawkmoth to find them but there is no need for the propagation of this plant by seed. It dies down at the end of the season to a thread-like root which curls along in the soil often to a great depth and springs up the next year from all sorts of unexpected places. The bud takes on a curious twisted form, shown clearly in plate 11 (see also plate 10). The twist here is anti-clockwise and is followed also in the tendrils as they climb, often entwining on themselves with such a quick growth that they can attain eight or ten feet in a season.

Gerard commends it as "very fit to make shadows in arbors", but it does need a support for climbing. Country names for the plant are "great withywind", "hedge lily", "our lady's nightcap", "old man's nightcap", "hedge bell" and "campanelle".

BLACKTHORN *Prunus spinosa*

There are eighteen references to the thorn or brier in Shakespeare's works, and he uses the toothed, sharp, prickled thorny plants to denote trouble and difficulties "among the thorns and dangers of this world" (*King John* iv. 3).

The blackthorn illustrated in plate 3 blooms in March or April, making patches of white in the still wintry hedges. Because it often coincides with a period of cold weather, country folk speak of a "blackthorn winter", meaning that it may be cold now but spring is just round the corner.

BRAMBLE *Rubus fructicosus*

The common bramble or blackberry bush has the habit of bending over to the ground where it roots again at the end of the branch, thus forming another bush, and explains why brambles cover neglected ground so quickly. There are many kinds, and some botanists distinguish 400 species in this country. The flowers vary from white to pink, including double blooms, and some have so many prickles that they continue along the mid-rib of the leaf, while others are only downy. Many species have leaves which are white on the under side (as the one illustrated in plate 14).

Falstaff speaks of reasons as plentiful as blackberries (*Henry IV Part 1* ii. 4) and in *Troilus and Cressida* (v. 4) Thersites says that Ulysses is not worth a blackberry – both quotations indicating that blackberries were equally abundant even in Shakespeare's time.

Ellacombe tells a quaint legend of the origin of the bramble which he says is worth repeating. "The cormorant was once a wool merchant. He entered into partnership with the bramble and the bat, and they freighted a large ship with wool; she was wrecked and the firm became bankrupt. Since that disaster the bat skulks about till midnight to avoid his creditors, the cormorant is forever diving into the deep to discover its foundered vessel while the bramble seizes hold of every passing sheep to make up his loss by stealing the wool."

He also says that some of the cultivated brambles are worth growing in the garden, most of them introduced from other countries.

One from Nepal has bright silvery bark and amber-coloured fruit, from New Zealand we have one that is hardy in the south of England and appears apparently leafless, and another is a handsome plant from the Rocky Mountains. Some of these foreigners are very unlike the blackberry about which Falstaff speaks but it is interesting to note that all the berries of the Rosaceae order are good to eat.

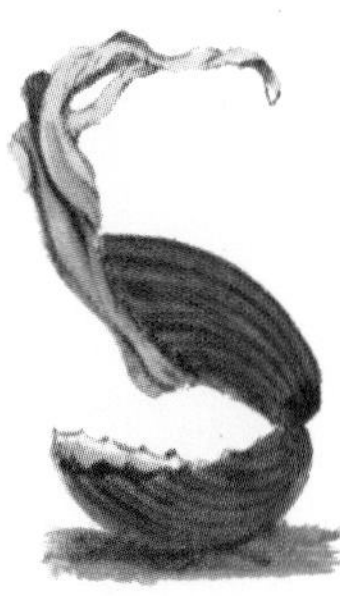

o I charm'd their ears
That calf like they my lowing follow'd through
Tooth'd **Briers**, sharp **Furzes** prickled **Gorse** & **Thorn**.

Tempest,
Act 4th Scene 1st

BURNET *Sanguishorba officinalis*

The Duke of Burgundy in *King Henry V* bemoans the state of France which was previously so fertile, the best garden in the world, and now has fallow fields full of weeds where the coulter rusts and the hedges are all overgrown. In plate 27 is illustrated the scented cowslip, burnet and clover, overpainted with the hateful weeds.

The plant the artist has chosen to represent burnet appears to be the great burnet, for the leaf behind is the rounded dentate one in contrast to the smaller pinnate leaves of the salad burnet (*Poterium sanguishorba*) which have the taste and smell of cucumber.

Poterium is derived from the Greek *poterion*, a drinking cup, according to Johns in *Flowers of the Field* because burnet was used for the preparation of cool-tankard, which possibly sounds better than it tasted. The Latin gives *sanguin* for blood and *sorbeo* for to staunch and with the old name bloodwort this suggests its possible use as a styptic.

Francis Bacon, who was contemporary with Shakespeare, valued it as a salad herb and advised that it should be grown with thyme and mint "to give pleasure where you walk and tread".

The lesser burnet is valued as a forage plant for sheep who can crop it in the winter on dry calcareous pastures when other food is scarce.

BURS *Arctium pubens*

The burs in plate 27 are the whorls of bracts enclosing the seed heads of the common burdock, often associated with thistles and docks in waste places and neglected fields. The bracts have sharp awl-shaped tips which hook on to any material and cannot be shaken off. When the burs are attached to the coat of an animal the seeds are carried to a distance, which is how the plant is propagated. Shakespeare frequently alludes to this property. Celia remarks to Rosalind in *As You Like It* (i. 3): "They are but burs, cousin, thrown upon thee in holiday foolery; if we walk not in the trodden paths our very petticoats will catch them." And the sad Rosalind replies: "I could shake them off my coat; these burs are in my heart." Again, Lysander repulses Hermia: "Hang off, thou cat, thou bur" (*A Midsummer Night's Dream* iii. 2). As usual, however, Shakespeare also uses the word in a symbolic sense. Pandarus claims constancy for her kindred saying: "They are burs, I can tell you; they'll stick where they are thrown" (*Troilus and Cressida* iii. 2). And in *Measure for Measure* Lucio shows persistence when he insists on his company to the lane's end and tells the Friar: "I am a kind of bur; I shall stick" (*Measure for Measure* iv. 3).

CARNATION *Dianthus caryophyllus*

In Greek and Roman times the carnation, illustrated in plate 17, because of its round shape and lasting power, was considered the most suitable flower for use in garlands and coronets, hence its name which is derived from *coronae*. The first part of its botanical name comes from the Athenians who called it "Flower of Jove" and the second indicates its clove-like scent. It is not a plant native to this country but when it was introduced is not certain. Ellacombe thought it probably came over with the Normans for it is found to this day in the cracks and crannies of ancient castles both in this country and in Normandy. How soon it became a florist's flower is not apparent, but by Elizabethan times it was so popular that gardeners vied with each other to provide new varieties, pinks, picotees and cloves. Master Ralph Tuggie was known to have a garden at Westminster and some of the best carnations were named after him: "Master Tuggie's Princesse" and "Master Tuggie, his Gilloflower". Gerard wrote: "A great and large volume would not surfice to write of every one . . . of how every yeare, every climate, and countrey, bringeth forth new, such as have not heretofore bin written of."

CLOVER *Trifolium repens*

The white clover is illustrated in plate 27, with the green represented by the typical three leaves. Shakespeare's only mention of clover in the plays is in *Henry V* (v. 2) but it is generally agreed that the "honey-stalks" of *Titus Andronicus* (iv. 4) must refer to clover:

> With words more sweet and yet more dangerous
> Than bait to fish, or honey-stalks to sheep.

The *English Dialect Dictionary* gives it as a name for white clover, that is no longer used.

Whether the clover or the woodsorrel is the shamrock of St. Patrick cannot really be proved, but it seems certain that the clover is the "club" of a pack of cards, for "clover" is a corruption of "clava" (a club). In England we put a clover design on our playing cards and call it "clubs" while in France they have the same pattern and call it *trèfle*.

That strain again; it had a dying fall:
O, it came o'er my ear like the sweet south,
That breathes upon a bank of **Violets**
Stealing and giving odour.

Twelfth Night,
Act 1st Scene 1st

COLUMBINE *Aquilegia vulgaris*

The columbine with a blue flower can be found in the wild but as a cultivated flower it has many beautiful colours (plate 19). The name is supposed to come from the dove or pigeon (L. *columba*), because the spurs curve inwards and look like the arched necks of the birds, with rounded heads and half-opened wings below. The botanical name is sometimes said to mean a water-carrier or else to come from *aquila*, an eagle. Larger flowers have been developed by the introduction of red and yellow species from North America and a lavender one from the Rocky Mountains which is the State flower of Colorado. It has been recommended for culinary purposes but Gerard is sensibly cautious, the Vertues are "to decke the gardens of the curious", which is as well, for all the Ranunculaceae family are liable to be poisonous.

CORN

Shakespeare alludes to corn (plate 23) over twenty times. Most references are concerned with the growing of the crops, the difficulties caused by weeds and weather, and the work of harvesting. It is noticeable that selling, bargaining and transport are mentioned in the earlier plays, perhaps with memories of meeting the farmers in the Corn Market at Stratford.

It is quite interesting to note that Gerard grew "turkie corne", which we call maize. He carefully explains that it came not from Asia Minor but out of America and the adjoining islands by way of Spain. He managed to grow it "when the summer falleth out to be faire and hot; as my selfe have seen proof in my own garden", but having taken that trouble he does not think much of it: "a more convenient food for swine than for man."

COWSLIP *Primula veris*

The paigle or cowslip, the cuckoobud of Shakespeare (plates 12, 27), is found in open fields rather than in woods or coppices, or the shelter of the hedgerows preferred by its near relation the primrose.

Shakespeare mentions the flower no less than six times and always with a happy description of some detail he has noticed and delighted in. He observed the freckled flower, the bell shape, the five crimson drops in the bottom of the yellow flower, and the tall, erect bearing, reminiscent of the splendidly dressed attendants of Queen Elizabeth I, who were called pensioners. The flower is associated in *The Tempest* with Ariel who is small enough to lie in the cowslip's bell, and with Puck, who is told in *A Midsummer Night's Dream* to

> seek some dewdrops here,
> and hang a pearl in every cowslip's ear.
> (ii. 1)

As primulas and polyanthus we know the flowers in our gardens, but they were already useful in Elizabethan times, when they brought a welcome patch of colour to the knot gardens. The children of a previous generation used to enjoy gathering them to make cowslip balls, by placing the heads on to a piece of string stretched between two chairbacks, and when enough were balanced on the string it was tied up into a ball to be hung in the window where it would last for a considerable time.

CROW FLOWER

The buttercup illustrated in plate 20 for the crow flower has the rounded shape and the reflexed sepals of *Ranunculus bulbosus*, but it could equally well have been the common meadow buttercup or the creeping one, both of which flower in the early summer. Gerard says they "grow of themselves in pastures everie where" and calls them "floures of a glittering colour like gold", but he warns that they may be dangerous simples if taken in ignorance. Such a common and decorative flower has had many names in the past: gold cups, gilcups, gold knobs, crow-foot and butter-flowers.

The reference in *Hamlet* (iv. 7) is Shakespeare's only one to the crow flower and Ellacombe thought that the name could be applied to the ragged robin (*Lychnis flos-cuculi*) or alternatively to the wild hyacinth or bluebell because the crow flower is so named by the herbalists Turner and Lyte. The bluebell is a doubtful claimant as it is a spring flower and, as Ellacombe points out, Ophelia's madness occurred in the early summer because she could gather pansies, columbine and fennel while the violets had all faded.

PLATE 5

Cesario, by the **Roses of the Spring**,
By maidenhood, honor, truth, & everything,
I love thee so, that, maugre all my pride,
Nor wit, nor reason can my passion hide.

Twelfth Night,
Act, 3rd Scene, 1st

CROWN IMPERIAL *Fritillaria imperialis*

Gerard describes the crown imperial (plate 16) as a rare and strange plant, a native of Persia and the Far East, which came to Europe from Constantinople and derived its name from the crown of blooms surmounted by a tuft of leaves. Shakespeare, who knew that it bloomed with the oxlips, would have seen it in London gardens. There is a legend about the curious droplets of nectar that appear below each flower, which do not fall when shaken and if removed are soon replaced. The story goes that when Jesus walked in the Garden of Gethsemane all the flowers but one dropped their heads in sympathy. The crown imperial, which was then white and upturned, alone remained unbowed because of pride in its name. But when Jesus looked at it, shame took the place of pride and the flower-heads were bent with blushing colour and everflowing tears as we see them to this day.

DAFFODIL *Narcissus pseudo-narcissus*

In *The Winter's Tale*, one of the later plays which he wrote when he was dividing his time between London and his home at New Place, Stratford, Shakespeare describes vividly and beautifully:

> Daffodils, that come before the swallow dares, and take
> The winds of March with beauty . . .
> (iv. 3)

He would be familiar with the daffodil-sellers in the London streets mentioned by Gerard, who also said that the flowers grew in abundance in London gardens (plate 16), but somehow the song in the same play suggests that Shakespeare had seen the yellow fields of wild daffodils which are still quite often found west of Stratford.

> When daffodils begin to peer,
> With heigh, the doxy o'er the dale,
> Why then comes in the sweet o' the year;
> For the red blood reigns in the winter's pale (iv. 2)

The *Two Noble Kinsmen* contains the only other references to daffodils – "chaplets on their heads of daffodillies" – and to the narcissus legend of

> A fair boy certaine, but a foole
> To love himself – were there not maidens enough?
> (ii. 2)

DAISY *Bellis perennis*

The daisy in plate 12 (see also plates 19, 20) shows the touch of pink on the edges of the white corolla, which Shakespeare describes as "pied". He recommends in *Cymbeline* (iv. 2) a search for "the prettiest daisied plot", which recalls the old country saying that one should not plant the corn until you can put a foot to cover six daisies.

The "days-eye" loved by Chaucer gets its name from the Anglo-Saxon *daeges-eage*, the eye of the day, which goes to sleep at night and is the first to open in the morning.

There are not many days in the year when a daisy cannot be found for its season starts with the spring flowers and continues through the summer. When the sorrowing Ophelia made her garlands she included the daises with the summer flowers, although she said the violets had all faded since her father died.

Children to this day make garlands of daisies, still a favourite flower for they are always allowed to pick them from the lawns and meadows.

DARNEL *Lolium temulentum*

Darnel or wild rye which is illustrated in plate 23 is a plant which has entirely disappeared from our corn fields, fortunately so, because the seeds were difficult to remove and they produced a bad taste in the bread, causing headaches and giddiness, and could even be poisonous for some people.

> Want ye corn for bread?
> I think the Duke of Burgundy will fast,
> Before he'll buy again at such a rate;
> 'Twas full of darnel; do you like the taste?
> *Henry VI Part 1* (iii. 2)

M ercifull heaven!
Thou rather, with thy sharp and sulphurous bolt,
Splitt'st the unwedgeable and gnarled **Oak**,
Than the soft **Myrtle**.

Measure for Measure,
Act, 2nd Scene 7.

DOCK *Rumex*

There are many kinds of docks with their familiar seedy stems frequenting the damp ditches of the hedgerows, covering many waste places and an unwanted weed in many gardens. Apart from the quotation accompanying plate 27, the only other time it is mentioned is in *The Tempest* (ii. 1) when jeering remarks are made about an ideal island: "He'd sow it with nettle seed, or docks, or mallows."

Ellacombe says an old name was "patience", supposed to be a corruption for "passions", but Gerard assumes this to be a separate variety called monks rhubarb, often still found in abbey grounds where it had been planted for the sake of the root which in colour and taste is like rhubarb. The root with aniseed and licorice and other herbs "purifieth the bloud and makes young wenches look faire and cherry-like".

EGLANTINE *Rosa eglanteria*

The word eglantine (plates 10, 21) is probably derived from the Latin *acus*, meaning a needle or sharp thorn, but it is not used much now and we call the plant the sweet briar. It gives out a pleasant and characteristic fragrance at dusk, particularly from the foliage which has special scent cells under the leaves.

ELM *Ulnus*

The elm mentioned in the quotation from *A Midsummer Night's Dream* with plate 11 is in the scene where Bottom with the rough furred donkey head is entwined by the loving arms of Titania. Shakespeare has noticed that the elm trunk has a rough corky bark, deeply fissured and of a dark grey, not unlike the texture and colour of a donkey's coat.

The tree blossoms in the early spring before the leaves come and immediately drops a great number of discs, each containing a seed, shown by the artist on the right of the picture. Fortunately the tree grows more easily by suckers for the elm disease has removed most of the trees in England, but in Shakespeare's time they would have been a feature of the landscape, in his part of the country especially.

FENNEL *Foeniculum vulgare*

Fennel (plate 19) is an aromatic pot-herb from the coasts of the Mediterranean but cultivated here from early days. Some authorities consider the name comes from its hay-like smell from the Latin *foenum* (hay). The feathery leaves are used for flavouring fish and the seeds taste a little like aniseed. It was evidently eaten with fish in Shakespeare's time. Falstaff says in a tavern in Eastcheap: "And a' plays at quoits well, and eats conger and fennel."

Here there is probably a further implication in the word "fennel", clear to the audiences of that day but lost to us.

FLOWER-DE-LUCE

Lilies of all kinds,
The flower-de-luce being one.
The Winter's Tale (iv. 3)

Opinions vary about this reference to the flower (plate 16), which in the four other places in which Shakespeare mentions it, clearly relates to the heraldic use of the iris in the French *fleur de lys* or *fleur de St. Louis*.

FUMITE *Fumus terrae*

This is fumitory (plate 23), a wild plant fairly common on the untreated borders of arable land. It has a dainty head of flowers, pink deepening to a purplish hue at the tips and appearing to be set at right angles to the stem. There are a number of theories about the derivation of its name but it is an ancient one and appears as *fumiter* in early manuscripts. The Latin easily becomes fumitory and means smoke of the earth. Some say the flowers give the impression of smoke as they grow and some that the colour of the leaves could be considered a smoky green. Others suggest that the smoke is in the scent and yet others that it is the juice of the stem that like smoke brings tears to the eyes.

It is mentioned again by the Duke of Burgundy when he bemoans the neglected fields of France.

Her fallow leas
The darnel, hemlock, and rank fumitory
Doth root upon.
Henry V (v. 2)

Presumably Shakespeare had seen it growing luxuriantly and had remarked on its strong smell, for he twice calls it "rank".

id her steal into the pleached bower,
Where **Honeysuckles** ripen'd by the sun,
Forbid the sun to enter like favorites
Made proud by princes, that advance their pride,
Against that power that bred it.

Much ado about Nothing
Act, 3rd Scene 1st

GILLIFLOWERS

There is some doubt whether "streak'd gilliflowers" are the variegated carnation or the wallflower which also had that name. The artist has painted both in plate 17. Gilliflower was often used as a general term for scented garden flowers and it can be found in old herbals applied to what we now call stocks and sweet williams.

The wild wallflower, *Cheiranthus chieri*, is yellow, the emblem of fidelity in misfortune. It is grown in our gardens in many shades of red, pink or yellow. The deep red ones used to be grown commerically; the colour obtained from the petals made a good dye before the production of synthetic ones.

Shakespeare's knowledge of gardening is well illustrated in the conversation in *The Winter's Tale* following the mention of "carnations and streak'd gilliflowers". Perdita cares not to get slips of these for she says she has not the art to get the piedness or streaks which she thinks are trying to add to nature. Then she is told that propagating plants by the methods of cuttings, grafting or hybridization is still nature's way, for nature makes the growth. Shakespeare also describes pruning, weeding, manuring, blights and frosts. Surely he must have found time to be concerned with a garden and the work entailed, perhaps at his house in New Place Stratford, if not also when visiting in London.

GORSE *Ulex europeaus*

The gorse or furze covers the hills with scented yellow blossom in early spring, but other varieties, such as the smaller *Ulex minor*, illustrated in the same plate (plate 3) are in bloom as late as October. This lengthening of the flowering season of gorse probably accounts for the saying that when gorse is out of blossom kissing's out of fashion.

HAREBELL *Endymion nonscriptus*

The harebell of Shakespeare (plate 21) is undoubtedly the wild hyacinth or bluebell, for although the name is applied differently in various parts of the country, in the south of England it is used for the beautiful blue flowers that carpet the woods and many roadsides in the late spring. Gerard refers to its curious botanical name ("the unwritten hyacinth") and recommends the juice of the bulb "to set the feathers upon arrowes instead of glew". He also advises its use when mixed with white wine to "hinder or keepe backe the growth of haires".

The likeness Shakespeare gives to "azured veins" is reminiscent of the slender stem which, when growing in the open hedgerows, takes on a tinge of blue very like the delicate blue of blood when the veins are seen through the skin.

HARLOCH

There is a difference of opinion here also about the plant that Shakespeare has mentioned. It appears in the different folios as hoar-docks, hardokes, and hardocks. Ellacombe considers it to be burdock, but Rhode and others support the view that it is charlock, the wild mustard, which is illustrated in plate 23. This plant grows with the other plants that King Lear gathered, and still appears as a field weed or on waste ground. Charlock (*Sinapis arvensis*) is a cruciferae related to the plant that provides mustard for the table. Both plants shine in the field with an exceptionally bright yellow glow.

HAWTHORN *Cretaegus monogyna*

The hawthorn (plate 14) variously called the may tree, the haythorne or quickset, takes its botanical name from the Greek *cratos*, meaning strong. Its flowering is the sign that tells us that winter is really past and summer is fairly begun; we even have the saying about not casting a clout till the may is out. The hawthorn gives berries in the autumn which we call "haws" (haw or hay is the old word for hedge) and grows so thickly that even a single tree in an exposed spot was said to give good shelter or shade for shepherds.

> Gives not the hawthorn-bush a sweeter shade
> To shepherds looking on their silly sheep
> Than doth a rich embroider'd canopy?
> *Henry VI Part III* (ii. 5)

And in *A Midsummer Night's Dream* Quince suggests that the hawthorn brake with its thick cover would make a suitable tiring house for the actors.

he seasons alter; hoary headed frosts
Fall on the fresh lap of the **Crimson Rose**;
And on old Hyems chin and icy crown
An odorous chaplet of sweet **Summer Buds**
Is, as in mockery, set.

Midsummer Night's Dream,
Act, 2nd Scene, 2nd

HEMLOCK *Conium maculatum*

This is a word given loosely to many members of the Umbelliferae family such as cow parsley and wild carrot. It is doubtful if Shakespeare would have included the true hemlock with the corn weeds (plate 23) for it is very poisonous and also prefers to grow in damp ditches or on the riversides rather than in cornfields.

In *Macbeth* (iv. 1) he does surely mean the foetid-smelling hemlock, as an ingredient of the witches' brew. That the "root of hemlock digged in the dark" would have had special strength if so produced, was commonly believed in those days, and had been since ancient times. According to Rhode there may be some foundation for this theory.

HOLLY *Ilex aquifolium*

Holly (plate 13) of the cheerful song in *As You Like It* (ii. 1) may have taken its name from "holy" and its association with the decoration of churches, but on the other hand it could have come from "haulm" or "holm". The Latin name suggests its form, the sharp spikes of the leaves. It grows in this country almost anywhere, under trees in the woods, as an impregnable hedge found in a garden or as an isolated tree in a hedge. The smugglers of the south coast used them as marker trees for direction inland and many a holly tree can be seen standing alone on the hills where "it outdares the winter's cold".

Shakespeare only mentions it once, in his song of Christmas cheer. In his knowledge of and fondness for flowers in season he would hardly have approved of the flowers we now have available all the year round:

> At Christmas I no more desire a rose
> Than wish a snow in May's new-fangled mirth,
> But like of each thing that in season grows.
> *Love's Labour's Lost* (i. 1)

HONEYSUCKLE *Lonicera periclymenum*

The lines accompanying the honeysuckle in plate 7 (see also plate 11) are from *Much Ado About Nothing* and are spoken in a garden where Hero asks Margaret to persuade Beatrice to hide in a honeysuckle bower, planning that she will overhear their conversation about how much Benedict loves Beatrice.

It is interesting to note that they walk along an alley or pathway in an orchard which has an arbour or bower, indicating that the orchards of those days were planted as gardens for enjoyment and not merely for the provision of fruit. The bower is thick enough to hide Beatrice and later in the scene she is "couched in the woodbine coverture". Here Shakespeare has clearly used the words honeysuckle and woodbine for the same plant. Ellacombe considers that honeysuckle could have meant the flower and that the name woodbine applied to the plant generally. Gerard is in agreement for he heads his chapter "Woodbine or Honeysuckle". Again woodbine was the word but surely it was the scented honeysuckle that covered Titania's bank of wild thyme (plate 10)? Ellacombe explains that in the earlier writings the name woodbine was given very loosely to almost any creeping or climbing plant. In an Anglo-Saxon Vocabulary of the eleventh century it was applied to wild clematis and other writers suggest ground ivy and convolvulus. After Shakespeare's time the words were again used confusedly which explains why the artist has clearly painted bindweed or convolvulus for woodbine in plate 11, and as summer buds in plate 8 and possibly also in plate 10. It is doubtful if bindweed would make such a thick hedge as the honeysuckle in the pleached bower.

"Pleached" means interwoven or wreathed. It is related to the words "plath" or "wreth" which describe a method of hedging by bending down the twigs and half splitting the branches to encourage a thick lower growth, a pleasant job for countrymen in winter for the cuttings make cheerful fires. These hedges will stand extreme cold and last much longer than the ones made by modern machinery which merely level the tops of the shrubs.

Another reference to pleached hedges comes in *Henry V* (v. 2) when Burgundy bemoans the infertility of France due to wars: "her hedges even pleached, wildly over grown."

The honeysuckle has been the emblem of firm and constant affection for when it climbs a tree or bush it entwines with such sure grip that the mark can usually be seen in the branch which supports it. Chaucer gave the crown of woodbine to those who were constant in love:

> And tho that weare chaplets on their hede
> Of fresh woodbine, be such as never were
> To love untrue in word, thought, ne dede.

There are two opposite leaves which endeavour always to face the sun, and this causes the plant to have the clockwise twist characteristic of many climbers. We have many varieties growing in our gardens, some with an earlier time of blossoming, some with brighter colours, but none so sweet-smelling as the hedgerow honeysuckle. The pale yellow flower has a deep pink tinge when in bud, which appears to burst open at dusk to send forth the perfume, attracting the hawk-moth with the long proboscis needed to reach the

PLATE 9

et mark'd I where the bolt of Cupid fell;
It fell upon a little western flower,
Before milk-white, now purple with love's wound,
And maidens call it, Love-in-idleness.

Midsummer Night's Dream,
Act, 2nd Scene, 2nd

honey and so fertilise the plant. Gerard describes a double honeysuckle in his garden and advises that "the floures steeped in oile, set in the sun, are good to unwind a body that is bemused and grown very cold".

Honeysuckle is mentioned again in quite a different context. In *Henry IV Part 2* (ii. 1) Mistress Quickly calls Falstaff a "honeysuckle vilain". This may be a play upon words, he having refused to pay "the hundred mark" he owes. She also calls "the arrant malmsy-nose knave Bardolph" a "honey-seed rogue". This could refer to the seeds of honeystalks and not honeysuckle, for the flower of clover is rounded and can be pinky-red.

Idle Weeds

The artist has painted a number of plants under this heading in plate 23. In the centre is the blue cornflower (*Centaurea cyanus*), cultivated now as a garden plant and seldom seen in the corn, where its tough stalks would blunt the scythes. Other names were blue bonnet, blue cap and blewbottle.

Corn cockle, *Lychnis githago*, is the pink star-like flower illustrated on the left of the plate. It was another plant like darnel, with seeds impossible to remove from the grain and is hardly ever seen now.

Another idle weed in the picture is the white daisy-like flower which is corn feverfew or wild camomile.

Iris *Iris pseudoacorus*

Shakespeare knew the yellow iris or water flag for he describes it in *Antony and Cleopatra* (i. 4) swaying back and forth with the movement of the stream. This is an example where in a few simple words Shakespeare brings in the character of the Elizabethan countryside and yet keeps the foreign scene, for the flags could easily be rushes or any long-leaved water plant.

The mauve iris pictured in plate 16 would be *Iris xiphiodes*, known as the English iris, but perhaps attributed to this country in error. According to Frances Perry in *Flowers of the World* it came from the Pyrenees to the port of Bristol where it flourished so well in the vicinity that Dutch bulb merchants obtained their first supplies there, and naturally they thought it was a native of Britain.

Gerard, who definitely considered the floure-de-luce to be an iris, says there are many kinds, some great and some small, some of many colours mixed, and he says of the yellow water flag: "although it be a watery plant yet being planted in gardens it prospereth well."

Ivy *Hedera helix*

As a wild plant ivy is found in Europe, Asia, and Africa but is not indigenous to America, and there are many beautiful variegated species grown in our gardens today. It is a symbol of lasting friendship, doubtless because it clings so tightly to the tree or building on which it climbs. Ivy has a bad name for damaging trees but it is probably only the soft sappy branches that suffer, and the "barky fingers" of the elm would come to no harm. It has the curious habit of changing the shape of its leaves. On the climbing stems they are the typical five-lobed kind and then when the plant is established it becomes bushy, the leaves are ovate and it produces flowers. Both kinds are illustrated in plate 11. The flowers come in the autumn and are a boon to the bees late in the year, producing black berries "by Lammastide". Ivy is often associated with holly for Christmas decorations and is a native plant known well by Chaucer, "the pallid ivie building his own bowre." Shakespeare mentions it three times for its clinging property and once in *The Winter's Tale* (iii. 3) when the shepherd looks for two sheep which may be "by the sea-side browsing of ivy".

There was an old custom of hanging a bush of ivy outside a tavern to indicate the good cheer to be had within. Hence came the saying "good wine needs no bush".

Kecksies

This is undoubtedly pictured as the thick hollow stem lying across the painting (plate 27). The kecksies, kecks or kex, are the names given to any umbelliferae stems but in particular that of the cow parsley or hemlock when it lingers in the hedge without leaves, flowers or fruit. In *English Wild Flowers* by J.T. Burgess, dated before 1878, it is said that this word is peculiar to the Midland shires.

Ladies' Smock *Cardamine pratensis*

This flower (plate 12), "all silver-white", certainly adds a sheen to the meadows in early spring and when in profusion looks at a distance like a sheet spread over the fields. Some have suggested that this explains the name, and recalls the days when women used to spread their smocks on the grass to bleach in the sun. The alternative name is cuckoo-flower, for they bloom when the sound of the cuckoo is heard in the woods and meadows.

The pure white variety is rare, and the dainty flower when fully open usually shows tints of pink and pale mauve, but still retains its silver sheen.

PLATE 10

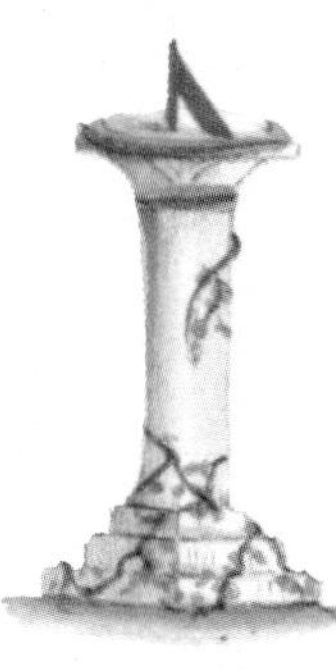

know a bank whereon the **Wild-Thyme** blows,
Where **Oxlips** & the nodding **Violet** grows,
Quite overcanopied with lush **Woodbine**,
With sweet **Musk-roses** & with **Eglantine**.

Midsummer Night's Dream,
Act. 2nd Scene, 2nd

LAVENDER *Lavandula vera*

Lavender (plate 15) has that fresh clean smell that one associates with linen which has come from a cupboard scented with lavender bags. Frequently in the past a hedge would be planted on which to spread the washing to dry, and a laundress was called a *lavendre* in Elizabethan times. The dried lavender stems were often burnt in a sick-room to clear the air, and this was also the purpose of growing lavender in pots on window sills. Lavender is often mentioned for its scent but seldom for its taste. "Hot" is the right word for it has a strong flavour a little like the mints.

LILY *Lilium*

The lily and the rose (plate 25) were associated together several times by Shakespeare. Both have been cultivated down the years from ancient times so that we now have both plants in divers colours and form.

> The colour in thy face
> That even for anger makes the lily pale,
> And the red rose blush at her own disgrace.
> *Lucrece* (477)

> Their silent war of lilies and of roses
> *Lucrece* (71)

> The air hath starved the roses in her cheeks,
> And pinch'd the lily tincture of her face.
> *Two Gentlemen of Verona* (iv. 4)

> Nor did I wonder at the lily's white
> Nor praise the deep vermilion of the rose
> Sonnet xcviii

The lily vies with the rose to be the favourite garden flower, but as it is more difficult to grow successfully it is not found in our gardens so often as the rose. It does not grow wild in this country, a fact Gerard does not seem to have appreciated for he writes: "There be sundry sortes of lilies, whereof some be wilde or of the field, and others tame or of the garden." Shakespeare would have been familiar with the various species described by Gerard, the white *Lilium candidum*, the scarlet Turk's Cap, *Lilium chalcedonium*, the orange *croceum*, and the martagon lily, newly introduced at that time, "given me by my loving friend Master James Garret, Apothecarie of London". It was so new that Gerard was not able to list the "Vertues".

The white lily is probably the oldest to be cultivated for it is found pictured on vases and other objects in Crete and Egypt dating centuries before Christ. The ancient world dedicated it to Juno for they said its whiteness was because it sprang from the spilling of her milk on to the earth. Later its purity and sweet perfume made it a symbol of the Virgin Mary and it appeared in many paintings in churches and monasteries, hence it became known as the Madonna Lily. Chaucer called it "Heven's Lilie".

By Elizabethan times it was generally accepted by artists, sculptors and poets as the unrivalled symbol of elegance and purity. Shakespeare mentions the flower nearly thirty times but always he refers to some such quality rather than a feature he has noticed in its form or growth, whereas in the wild flowers he has observed many such details in the "freckled cowslip" and the "nodding violet". He speaks of the "unsullied lily", "a most unspotted lily", "fresh lily" and "O sweetest, fairest lily". Its whiteness is remarked in *A Midsummer Night's Dream* (iii. 1): "Most radiant Pyramus, most lily-white of hue", and "she is as white as a lily" in *Two Gentlemen of Verona* (ii. 3). It is often used as a synonym for white: "These lily lips", "Those lily hands", "Thou lily-livered boy" and "She locks her lily fingers one in one", "Her lily hand, her rosy cheek lies under."

Perhaps the only time there is a suggestion of disapproval is the description in Sonnet xciv:

> For sweetest things turn sourst by their deeds;
> Lilies that fester smell far worse than weeds.

This was surely recalled from an actual garden experience, and also:

> Fresh tears
> Stood on her cheeks as dothe the honey-dew
> Upon a gather'd lily almost wither'd.
> *Titus Andronicus* (iii. 1)

And Salisbury commenting on King John being once again crowned:

> To guard a title that was rich before
> To gild refined gold, to paint the lily
> . . . or add another hue
> Unto the rainbow . . .
> Is wasteful and ridiculous excess.
> *King John* (iv. 2)

PLATE 11

Sleep thou and I will wind thee in my arms
Fairies begone and be all ways away,
So doth the **Woodbine**, the sweet **Honeysuckle**
Gently entwist- the female **Ivy** so
Enrings the barky fingers of the **Elm.**

Midsummer Nights Dream,
Act 4th Scene 1st

LONG PURPLES

This is probably the name for any of the purple orchids found in the fields and woods. It is difficult to decide which one is pictured in plate 20 but the spots on the leaves suggest the early purple *Orchis macula* which flowers in shady places from April to May. The green-winged orchid *morio* is plentiful in many moist meadows where there are often hybridized examples of these purple flowers. Gerard calls them all "satyrions" as they were supposed to have been the unholy plants of satyrs.

Shakespeare describes them as "long purples, that the liberal shepherds give a grosser name, but our cold maids do dead men's fingers call them".

This probably refers to the palmate roots of some of the species, but Ellacombe, writing from a rectory in mid-Victorian England, suggests that the other names which are mentioned should not be inquired too curiously: "they are given in all their 'liberality' and 'grossness' in the old herbals but as common names they are fortunately extinct." These orchids have two tubers formed from the rootstock, one to supply the plant with necessities for growth, the other to receive supplies for future use. In *The English Botany* by J. Sowerby (1799), it is stated that from the time of the ancient Greeks the resemblance of these twin tubers to a pair of testicles gave them an unwarranted reputation as an aphrodisiac. A thin gruel was made from the roots and was sold as salep or saloop on the street stalls of London, which was very popular and considered to be very nutritious.

LOVE-IN-IDLENESS *Viola tricolor*

We know the flower as pansy; the purple mark appears on the petals of this variety in contrast to *Viola arvensis* which is smaller and quite pale. Both are found wild in the northern hemisphere. Love-in-idleness Shakespeare again called it in *The Taming of the Shrew*, and by that name it is said to be known in Warwickshire and the Midlands to this day. "Idleness" in this sense has the meaning "in vain" or "to no purpose" which hardly accords with the other popular name, "heartsease".

In *A Midsummer Night's Dream* Oberon tells the charming story of how Cupid's love shaft missed its mark and fell upon a little milk-white flower giving its juice magical powers through the purple love wound, and Shakespeare also called it "cupid's flower" when Oberon gives instructions for the antidote to the charm (plate 9). One wonders why he termed it a "little western flower". There is no mention in Gerard's *Herball* of pansy or viola so possibly it did not grow near London – nor in a wood near Athens. Warwickshire could be considered to be westerly but perhaps in his travels Shakespeare came further west to see this flower?

Ophelia offered pansies for thoughts (see plate 19). This name may come from the French *penser* and we have the expression "in a pensive mood". Italians call it *flammola* ("little flame") or "herb trinity". The original Anglo-Saxon word seems to have been *bonewort* which is not so poetical as the many fanciful names this small flower has acquired, some descriptive as "three-faces-under-a-hood", others lightly associated with invitation to love: "cuddle-me-to-you", "tickle-my-fancy", "kiss-me-ere-I-rise", "jump-up-and-kiss-me", "pink-of-my-john", becoming "pinkeney-john" and from America "johny-jump-ups" or merely "johnnies".

MARIGOLD *Calendula officinalis*

Ellacombe says there are at least three plants claiming to be the marigold of Shakespeare: the buttercup-shaped marsh marigold, the corn marigold like a chrysanthemum, or the garden marigold sometimes known as "golds". The artist has chosen in plate 15 the last one for the bright orange flower that follows the sun till bedtime and this one also has culinary properties. It adds flavour to stews and colour to cheese, and can be an ingredient in salads. Shakespeare also mentions its obedience to the sun in *Lucrece*:

> Her eyes, like marigolds had sheathed their light,
> And canopied in darkness sweetly lay,
> Till they might open to adorn the day.

But in the song in *Cymbeline* (ii. 3), he describes:

> Winking marybuds begin
> To ope their golden eyes.

This lovely song surely indicates a water plant and not a garden one, so here it really may be the marsh marigold (*Caltha palustris*), an equally bright and beautiful plant variously known as kingcup, water cowslip and mayflower. Marigolds with violets, a vivid contrast in colour, were strewn by Marina on Thaisa's grave "while summer days do last" (*Pericles* iv. 1). Marigolds or calendulas come with the spring flowers and often last sparingly until Christmas, hence the name, the flower that appears in all the calends.

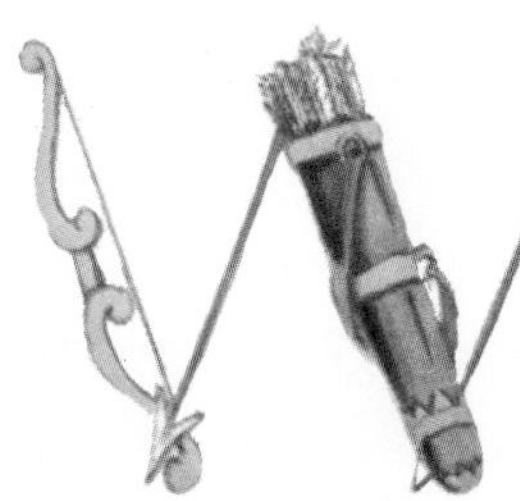

hen **Dasies** pied, and **Violets** blue,
And **Ladiesmocks** all silver white,
And **Cuckoo-buds** of yellow hue,
Do paint the meadows with delight.

Loves Labour's Lost,
Act, 5th Scene, 2nd

MARJORAM *Origanum majoranum*

Marjoram (plate 15) or origanum is still used as a garden herb and came originally from the south of Europe. Lyte suggests several kinds to grow but Gerard says origany in wine is a remedy for "bitings and stingings of venomous beasts and also cureth them that have drunke opium or the juice of black poppy or hemlock".

The name is used by Shakespeare as a pass word – "sweet majorum" – in *King Lear* (iv. 6). Again in *All's Well That Ends Well* (iv. 5) "she was the sweet marjorum of the salad", followed by a humorous but apt remark that they are not salad herbs but nose-herbs.

MINT *Mentha*

Mints (plate 15) are usually spoken of in the plural, probably because there are many different garden kinds and several wild ones. *Mentha aquatica* is the one the artist has painted, the wild one with the round flower head. Gerard grew them in his garden and also knew the wild ones. He recommends them "to be good against the stinging of wasps and bees, if the place be rubbed therewith". Parkinson describes the various mints to grow and suggests that mints with balm and other herbs used in a bath will strengthen the nerves and sinews.

MISTLETOE *Viscum album*

Shakespeare only makes one reference to mistletoe (plate 30) which is the only species in this country of the large family Loranthacae, consisting of usually tropical small shrubs which live and thrive attached to a host by means of modified roots. One authority suggests "mist" means "different" and "tan" a "twig", giving the name of the plant which is so unlike the tree on which it grows. In Shakespeare's time this apparent growth without a seed and for no observable reason caused the mistletoe to be treated with some awe and much distrust. It was associated with the Druids who venerated the bush and claimed that it had magical powers, such as the gift of prophetic dreams, charms against witches and remedies for all sorts of poisons and diseases. Actually the seed is in a viscous berry and the plant can be propagated by its ability to stick to the bark and remain to germinate if on the under-side of a branch. It grows mostly in the south attached to trees of apple, pear, poplar, lime and very rarely oak. There is a Norse legend that Balbur was slain by an arrow made of mistletoe, hence came the belief that the plant was sacred. When enemies met in the forest and happened to see the mistletoe they would make a truce for the day. From this came the custom of hanging mistletoe over the door as a sign of peace and of giving the kiss as a sign of friendship.

MOSS *Musci*

It is noticeable that Shakespeare (plates 21, 30) leaves out the autumn flowers in his choice for the grave (*Cymbeline* iv. 2) and then mentions moss which will last all winter. This is because the warm-coloured flowers we associate with the autumn, rudbeckias, phlox, stocks, asters and michaelmas daisies, dahlias and chrysanthemums, had not yet been brought to this country from abroad. John Tradescant, the elder, was just contemporary with Shakespeare but it was after his death in 1616 that the two Tradescants, father and son, brought so many plants to this country, in particular the fall plants from North America. Moss in Shakespeare's day included all the low-growing and apparently flowerless carpet plants which are now divided into many families of mosses and lichens.

He uses the word idle to describe the moss in *Comedy of Errors* (ii. 2), "dross usurping ivy, brier, or idle moss", perhaps in contrast to the fecundity of ivy and briers. But moss is by no means idle (or of little value) when Hotspur speaks of the moss-grown steeples and towers in *Henry IV Part I* (iii. 1), or "an oak whose boughs were Moss'd with age" in *As You Like It* (iv. 3).

The use of moss through the ages is beautifully described by Ruskin in *Modern Painters*. "The first mercy of the earth, veiling with hushed softness its dentless rocks . . . gathered like flowers for a chaplet or love token . . . the soft mosses and grey lichens take their watch by the headstone."

MUSK ROSE *Rosa arvensis*

The musk rose of the hedgerows, sometimes called the trailing rose, has dark stems and curled white petals as illustrated in plate 10. Its flowers, particularly the stamens, release a musk-like perfume towards dusk when the heavy scent hangs on the air all through a calm night. The *Rosa moschata*, which has pure white flowers, is another variety considered by many to be Shakespeare's "musk-rose" of *A Midsummer Night's Dream*. He rightly plants it in Titania's bower for it was the only climbing rose known in his day – the eglantine never grows very high. The musk rose was cultivated in Europe for centuries but originally came from the Himalayas.

eigh, ho! sing heigh, ho! unto the **Green Holly**:
Most friendship is feigning, most loving mere folly:
Then, heigh ho! the holly!
This life is most jolly.

As you like it.
Act 2nd Scene 7th

MYRTLE *Myrtus communis*

This is a small shrub, illustrated in plate 6, with white flowers full of stamens and small fragrant leaves, native to the Mediterranean countries. It was probably introduced to England not long before Shakespeare's time, when it was looked upon as an elegant plant of refined beauty, for it only grows in sheltered places and preferably by the sea. In the warm south-west, in Devon and Cornwall, it can be seen as a large blossoming tree in gardens near the coast.

Myrtle was dedicated to Venus, the goddess of love, an association which we still keep in the traditional use of myrtle as a spray in bridal bouquets, and groves of myrtle were planted round the temples of Venus in Greece. In the poem *The Passionate Pilgrim* xi.

> Venus with young Adonis sitting by her,
> Under a myrtle shade began to woo him.

and in *Venus and Adonis*

> Then sad she hasteth to a myrtle grove.

There is also mention in *The Passionate Pilgrim* of a kirtle embroidered all over with leaves of myrtle.

However, the most beautiful reference to myrtle is in *Antony and Cleopatra*: "as . . . the morn-dew on the myrtle leaf", a lovely picture created again by Shakespeare in *Lucrece*:

> As in the morning's silver-melting dew
> Against the golden splendour of the sun.

NETTLE *Lamium*

In plate 20 the white dead nettle, unrelated to the stinging nettle (*Urtica*), is illustrated as part of Ophelia's garland. The yellow dead nettle is often called archangel, reputedly because it has the virtue of looking like a nettle but without the sting. Gerard gives a curiously detailed account of where they could be found, i.e., "under the hedge on the left hand as you go from the village of Hampstead, near London, to the church and in the wood thereby". It is very doubtful, even with this clear description, whether there would be any to find at Hampstead now.

He also gives a recipe for the distilled water of the flowers "which is used to make the heart merry, to make a good colour in the face, and to refresh vitall spirits".

The nettle in plates 23 and 26 is not the one which Ophelia picked but the *Urtica dioica*, the stinging nettle. It is mentioned by Shakespeare a number of times, and invariably to describe that stinging quality of "goads, thorns . . . tails of wasps", expressed by the name *Urtica* which comes from *uro* (to burn). Nettle is etymologically the same word as needle but, while it is so named because of its connection with sewing, it is not the needle but the thread which was the original meaning. Nettles make a very good strong thread and nettle linen is reported to be very hard wearing. Very young nettles can be boiled as a vegetable and taste rather like spinach. Gerard explains that when withered or boiled "it stingeth not at all".

OAK *Quercus robus*

There is much of a legendary nature about the oaks of old England; with their stout trunks and very strong roots they are reputed to be able to last a thousand years. Shakespeare mentions the oak (plates 6, 18) in some form nearly thirty times, mostly with the character of steadfast strength: "the unwedgeable", "the rock, the oak, not to be windshaken", "Jove's stout oak". He gives many a picture of the tree often as a winter silhouette "bare to every stem", "gnarled" and "knotty", "boughs mossed with age and high top bald with dry antiquity". The spreading branches tend to assume a tortuous almost zigzag form, noted by Shakespeare as "knees of knotted oak". He also mentions the "hardest-timbered oak" and its use for ships, "ribs of oak" and the "seeling up as close as oak". Oak trees are often used as a meeting place, Herne's oak in *The Merry Wives of Windsor* and Duke's oak in *A Midsummer Night's Dream*. The leaves are traditionally used as garlands for the victor: "the best man i' the field, and for his meed was brow bound with the oak" (*Coriolanus* ii. 2). In addition acorns or mast are mentioned several times, including: "All their elves for fear creep into acorn-cups and hide them there" (*A Midsummer Night's Dream* ii. 1), an indication of the supposed size of the fairies.

Plate 6 shows the pendant male flowers and an oak-apple, a gall formed by an insect, traditionally worn to signify support for Charles II because he escaped from Cromwell's troops by hiding in the thick branches of an oak tree.

PLATE 14

There is a man haunts the forest, that abuses
our young plants with carving Rosalind
on their barks; hangs odes upon **Hawthorns**,
and elegies on **Brambles**; all, forsooth, deifying the
name of Rosalind.

As you like it,
Act, 3rd Scene. 2nd

OATS *Avena sativa*

The older English name was *haver*, quite possibly from the Latin name for oat, *avena*. The word was in use in Shakespeare's time and has survived in the north of England where oats are mostly grown (plate 2).

> Poor fellow, never joyed since the price of oats rose – it was the death of him.
> *Henry IV Part I* (ii. 1)

> When shepherds pipe on oaten straws.
> *Love's Labour's Lost* (v. 2)

OXLIP *Primula elatior*

The oxlip (plates 10, 16) is a more striking plant than either the cowslip or the primrose, to which it is closely related. It is found more often in open ground than in woodland and was a favourite in cottage gardens where it showed the umbel shape of the cowslip with blooms almost as large as the primrose. Shakespeare refers to "the bold oxlip" in *A Midsummer Night's Dream*, *The Winter's Tale* and *Two Noble Kinsmen.*

PANSY *see* Love-in-Idleness

PEAS *Pisum sativum*

Cultivated for fodder and as a vegetable, "peas" is a curious word, the singular of which is "pease", derived from *pisum*.

Shakespeare several times alludes to "pease" (plate 2), "peascod" and "squash" and carefully explains the meanings in *Twelfth Night* (i. 5) where Malvolio says:

> Not yet old enough to be a man, nor young enough to be a boy; as a squash is before 'tis a peascod, or a codling when 'tis almost an apple.

Thus squash is the young pod before the peas are formed and peascod is the unshelled pea, from "cod" meaning a bag.

Wild peas sometimes became big enough to shell and stories are told of people being saved from starvation by finding good plants on the sea shore. The plant has been very much altered by cultivation and does not seem to have been introduced as a garden plant much before Shakespeare's time for it was not in the old lists of garden plants. When first produced and imported from Holland they were termed "fit dainties for ladies, they came so far and cost so much".

POPPY *Papaver rhoeas*

The red corn poppy is the one illustrated in plate 22, but whether this was the small flower the juice of which Friar Lawrence gave to Juliet is open to doubt, for its narcotic properties are very weak. The opium poppy, *Papaver somniferum*, was known and cultivated in England long before Shakespeare's time but only as a garden ornament; the opium was, as now, imported from the East. The poppy mentioned by Iago, which induces drowsy sleep in *Othello* (iii. 3) is probably also the opium which is not red in colour, but larger, and lilac, white or pink.

The wild red poppy of the corn fields has the property of keeping its seed fertile below ground, so that when the soil is freshly turned it appears next year in a profusion of red blossoms, a sight often seen these days on the banks of newly made roads in England. This is why the poppies appeared on the battlefields in Flanders and have become a symbol of World War I. Perhaps the soldiers saw them with the sun shining through the delicate leaves above the mud, as Ruskin wrote of them in *Prosperina*: "The poppy is painted glass; it never glows so brightly as when the sun shines through it . . . always it is a flame, and warms the wind like a blown ruby."

It seems strange, however, that Shakespeare with his sense of colour and keen observation did not mention this conspicuous plant when he refers to the cereal corn twenty-three times in the plays and even lists all the other weeds of the corn (plate 23). This is explained when it is realized that it was not until eleven years after his death that John Tradescant in 1627 brought back to England the seeds of the vivid red flowers he saw on the island of Rhe opposite Rochelle. Hence we have the name *rhoeas* and from these plants was developed later the strain of shirley poppies. Gerard mentions a red poppy (*Papaver sylvestre*) and also *Papaver rhoeas*, but the latter is added in the amended edition by Thomas Johnson which was not printed till 1633.

ere's flowers for you!
Hot **Lavender, Mints, Savory, Marjoram;**
The **Marigold**, that goes to bed with the sun,
And with him rises weeping.

Winters Tale,
Act 4th Scene 3rd

PRIMROSE *Primula vulgaris*

The name of the primrose (plates 5, 16, 21) is derived from the old Italian word *primerole*, a diminutive of *primaverola* – from *flor di prima vera*, the first flower of spring.

> Primrose, first-born child of Ver
> Merry spring-time's harbinger
> *Two Noble Kinsmen* (Introductory Song)

Shakespeare mentions the primrose a number of times in the plays, often in connection with other spring flowers such as violets, cowslips and bluebells. His keen observation and botanical knowledge is evident in the reference in *The Winter's Tale* (iv. 3).

> Pale primroses
> That die unmarried, ere they can behold
> Bright Phoebus in his strength.

With vivid recollection of the primrose banks of his youth he has noticed that there are pin-eyed and thrum-eyed blooms, male and female, which need the help of insects for fertilisation, and their absence in very early spring tends to prevent this. Nevertheless, this dimorphism brings about many natural hybrids which were already around in Shakespeare's time, as we know from Gerard who mentions the double primrose, the cup-and-saucer and the "Jack-in-the-Green", with a curious frill below the yellow petals.

Shakespeare may have had other memories of a path through the woods when courting his wife at Shottery or on the way to his mother's home in Wilmcote, for he writes of "the primrose way" (*Macbeth* ii. 3) and of "the primrose path of dalliance" (*Hamlet* i. 3).

ROSE *Rosa*

There is no flower mentioned so often by Shakespeare as the rose (plates 8, 25, 28, 29). He uses it symbolically for its beauty, and also for both colour and perfume; he has knowledge of its growth, pruning and grafting; he alludes to its thorns, to canker and insects "that eat its leaves away". He must have been familiar with the gardens of London as well as those of the country-side for he mentions several distinct kinds, the red and white of the royal emblem, the musk rose, the Provencal rose, the Damask rose, and the variegated one we still know as *Rosa mundi*. It is encouraging that these old shrub roses are becoming more popular and can often be found growing in our gardens today.

> There will we make our beds of roses
> And a thousand fragrant posies.
> *Merry Wives of Windsor* (iii. 1)

The red roses can all be related back to the *Rosa rubra* introduced to Europe by travellers from south-east Asia where they were grown intensively by the ancient Greeks and Romans, and the Egyptians. There are records that the floors in Cleopatra's palace were covered inches deep with rose petals and they were even showered from the ceilings. Rose petal beds were made for guests to lie upon, hence the term "a bed of roses".

The Romans probably brought this rose to France and later the Crusaders as well. It was cultivated there not so much for its beauty but for its medicinal properties and for cosmetics. It came to this country as the French rose, *Rosa gallica*, which Shakespeare would have known as the Apothecary's rose. "Cakes of roses" were part of the stock-in-trade of the Apothecary in *Romeo and Juliet* (v. 1). Dried petals of this rose were much in demand for they retained their perfume longer than others. Potpourri was frequently made for it helped to reduce the musty smell in rooms of cottages and manor houses.

> Of their sweet deaths are sweeter odours made.
> Sonnet liv

Bowls of rose-water were provided at banquets where fingers were still habitually used.

> Let one attend him with a silver basin
> Full of rose-water and bestrew'd with flowers.
> *Taming of the Shrew* (Induction)

And from the same play (ii. 1) comes a delightful expression: "as morning roses newly washed with dew." The dew upon roses was supposed to make the best and most expensive cosmetics.

Gerard considered the rose "the most glorious floure of the world", and as usual in his *Herball* he valued it for its "Vertues". The distilled water and the sugar conserves he recommends for strengthening the heart, for giving sleep and putting into "junketting dishes, cakes, sauces and many other pleasant things giving a fine and delectable taste". Shakespeare also said: "Of all flowers methinks a rose is best" (*Two Noble Kinsmen* ii. 2). And we note "What though the rose has prickles? Yet 'tis plucked." (*Venus and Adonis*).

> Then will I raise aloft the milk-white rose
> With whose sweet smell the air shall be perfumed.
> *King Henry VI Part 2* (i. 1)

This last is clearly a description of the white rose of York but from whence it originated there seems to be some doubt. It may have been here already when the

PLATE 16

affodils,
That come before the swallow dares, and take
The winds of March with beauty; Violets dim,
But sweeter than the lids of Juno's eyes,
Or Cytherea's breath; pale Primroses,
bold Oxlips, and
The Crown-imperial, lilies of all kinds
The Flower-de-luce being one.

The Winters Tale,
Act 4th Scene 3rd

Romans came for there is an ancient tradition mentioned by Pliny that Albion was so named "either from its white cliffs or from the white roses with which it abounds".

It was obviously a garden rose by Tudor times. Gerard describes a double white rose growing in the hedges near his home in the north as abundantly as the briers grow in the southern parts. Ellacombe considers this to be the white rose of York, a double variety of *Rosa arvensis*.

> Your colour, I warrant you, is as red as any rose
> *King Henry VI Part 1* (ii. 4)

The red rose had been the rose of Lancaster for about two hundred years before the Wars of the Roses. In the time of Edward I it was introduced by Edmunde, Duke of Lancaster, who had enjoyed seeing it in the Provins district of France, where he had been sent to quell a riot. A large area of France was still in England's possession, and in the warmer climate the rose had been much cultivated and further developed into the double varieties. These red and white roses are mentioned many times by Shakespeare in the historical plays and also when combined as the versicolor. Probably he is thinking of the true York and Lancastrian rose in the following:

> One blushing shame, another white despair,
> A third, nor red nor white, had stol'n from both.
> Sonnet xcix

Although roses come now in many colours it is the red hue that we associate with the rose. We often say children have rosy red lips and when we speak of a child's rosy cheeks we do not mean they are pink or white. Nor did Shakespeare. He speaks of "rose cheeked youth", "rose-lipped cherubin" and "Your colour, I warrant, is red as any rose" (*Henry IV Part 2* ii. 4). But the fading of the cheeks is used to denote fear or sickness:

> The roses in thy lips and cheeks shall fade
> To paly ashes.
> *Romeo and Juliet* (iv. 1)

> Why is your cheek so pale?
> How chance the roses there do fade so fast?
> *A Midsummer Night's Dream* (i. 1)

There is an underlying sentiment that even the brightest scene has its dark side as the stem has its thorns and the flower has its canker,

> This thorn
> Doth to our rose of youth rightly belong,
> *All's Well That Ends Well* (i. 3)

> I know what thorns the growing rose defends
> *Lucrece* (492)

> Shame, like canker in the fragrant rose
> Doth spot the beauty of thy budding name.
> Sonnet xcv

There are nearly a hundred references to the rose and while many of these are used symbolically the rose is also spoken of as a plant.

> Roses have thorns and silver fountains mud,
> And loathsome canker lives in the sweetest bud.
> Sonnet xxxv

> When I have pluck'd the rose,
> I cannot give it vital growth again,
> It needs must wither. I'll smell it on the tree.
> *Othello* (v. 2)

> Superfluous branches
> We lop away, that bearing boughs may live.
> *Richard II* (iii. 4)

The different species are mentioned:

> With two Provincial roses on my razed shoes
> *Hamlet* (iii. 2)

> Gloves as sweet as damask roses
> *A Midsummer Night's Dream* (iii. 1)

Gerard describes the damask rose "of a pale red colour", and Shakespeare also alludes to the variegated damask:

> I have seen roses damask'd, red and white
> But no such roses see I in her cheeks.
> Sonnet cxxx

> Fair ladies mask'd are roses in their bud;
> Dismask'd, their damask sweet commixture shown,
> Are angels veiling crowds, or roses blown.
> *Love's Labour's Lost* (v. 2)

PLATE 17

he fairest flowers o'the season
Are our Carnations & streak'd Gilliflowers.

Winters Tale,
Act 4th Scene 3rd

ROSEMARY *Rosmarinus*

Of the many phrases from the plays that have come into our ordinary use this is one very often heard: "rosemary for remembrance" (plate 19). For this reason rosemary has been much used at funerals; in *Romeo and Juliet* the Friar says to the mourning Capulets:

> Dry up your tears, and stick your rosemary
> On this fair corse.
> (iv. 5)

It was also valued for its long-lasting properties. The leaves stay green and the scent remains strong on a sprig, but hardly enough to support the belief quoted by Ellacombe that a branch of rosemary in the hands of the dead would sprout and grow so much that in time it would cover the corpse in the coffin. From this, however, came the saying "keeping the memory green".

One might expect the name to mean the rose of Mary, but actually it comes from the Latin *rosmarinus* which indicates that it is a sea-loving plant. It is not a native of Britain but comes from the sea coasts of southern Europe where it is abundant. In a knot garden it would be a small well clipped hedge, but Sir Thomas More wrote that he allowed it to run over his garden walls for he had a great affection for it – so had his bees.

When it becomes a large shrub Parkinson remarks that the wood makes lutes and such like instruments, also carpenters' rules. It is recommended for many cures, as a hair tonic for baldness, as a pillow to promote sleep, for friendship in garlands at weddings, the ash of burnt twigs to relieve toothache, as decorations for dishes of meat and as a conserve to comfort the heart. Each year on April 23rd, St. George's Day, which is also Shakespeare's birthday, the people of Stratford wear a sprig of rosemary and carry wreaths of scented flowers and herbs in procession through the town.

RUE *Ruta graveolens*

Rue (plate 19) is a bitter herb with rather unusual small rounded leaves and a blue-green colour that makes a good contrast to other plants in the herb garden. It is a native, like rosemary, of the coasts of southern Europe. Ellacombe has explained that the bitterness leads to its other name, Herb of Grace, for we have the expression "to rue it", meaning to repent and hence to have grace. Perdita in the scene from *The Winter's Tale* first gives rosemary and rue to the visitors:

> These keep
> Seeming and savour all the winter long
> Grace and remembrance be to you both.
> (iv. 4)

In an early play (*Richard II*) it is used in the sense of pity. Although the Queen unkindly hopes the plants which the gardener grafts "may never grow", nevertheless he plans to:

> Set a bank of rue, sour herb of grace;
> Rue, even for ruth, here shortly should be seen
> In remembrance of a weeping queen.
> (iii. 4)

Its main use was for strewing the leaves in rooms to overcome evil odours. Rue also appears in heraldry in the Collar of the Order of the Thistle and in the arms of the Duke of Saxony.

RYE *Secale cereale*

Rye (plate 2) is, like wheat, not a British plant and its origin is not exactly known, but Ellacombe considers it came with its name from the region of the Caucasus. As a food plant it was not in good repute in Elizabethan times. Gerard says: "It is harder to digest than wheat, yet to rusticke bodies that can well digest it, it yields good nourishment." There is a song in *As You Like It* (v. 3):

> Between the acres of the rye
> These pretty country folks would lye.

In *The Tempest* (iv. 1) there is a description of harvest home which Shakespeare must actually have seen – and a further use for straw.

> You sunburnt sicklemen of August weary,
> Come hither from the furrow and be merry;
> Make holiday; your rye-straw hats put on.

hy should you want? Behold the earth hath roots;
Within this mile break forth a hundred springs:
The **Oaks** bear mast, the **Briers** scarlet hips;
The bounteous housewife nature, on each bush
Lays her full mess before you.

Timon of Athens,
Act 4th. Scene, 3rd.

SAMPHIRE *Crithmum maritimum*

Samphire, illustrated in plate 24, is a thick fleshy plant with strangely shaped leaves and a strong aromatic scent, which grows in rocky clefts on many of the hilly coasts of Britain. It was dedicated to Saint Peter because of its habitation and the association with *petra*, a rock, so the name is probably a corruption of the fisherman saint's name.

The picking of samphire for pickling has practically died out now but it was considered a great delicacy. The strong smelling leaves, stems and roots were collected in May, sprinkled with salt and preserved in vinegar to make a pickle, so popular that a peck of samphire was presented to a seventeenth-century surgeon as a sufficient fee for setting a broken arm.

In Shakespeare's time the gathering of samphire was a regular trade and a dangerous one; the collector sometimes hung from a rope, dangling in the air a distance down the cliff and in sight of the waves pounding on the rocks below. In our time the quantity required could easily be obtained without so much danger for, besides the fact that we now have rock-climbing equipment, it often grows in quite accessible positions on the sea coasts.

SAVORY *Satureia*

Savory (plate 15) is a native of southern Europe and was probably brought to England by the Romans for it is mentioned in the Anglo-Saxon recipes under the name of savorie. Parkinson recommends its use amongst the "farsing or farsetting herbs", meaning herbs for stuffing, a word still used in the expression "force-meat balls".

STRAWBERRY *Fragaria vesca*

The strawberry (plate 26) grown in England in the Elizabethan days was the wild one reputed to grow better in woodland. It was a popular belief that better plants are produced when grown near an inferior kind, such as the association of garlic with roses to improve their scent. Tusser in his *Five Hundred Points of Good Husbandry* (1577) recommends bringing in the wild strawberries from the woods:

> Wife, into thy garden, and set me a plot
> With strawberry roots the best to be got:
> Such growing abroade among thornes in the wood,
> Wel chosen and picked prove excellent good.

Bacon in his *Essay of Gardens* mentions that the fading leaves have a "most excellent cordiall smell", but this is not observable from the leaves of our cultivated species of strawberries. Besides the wild one they had the Virginian *Fragaria virginiana*, a native of North America and the parent of our scarlets, but the ones from Chile or California had not yet come over to provide the really good varieties for the gardens. In another historical play, *Richard III*, the Bishop of Ely provided strawberries from his garden for the King. Shakespeare tells of this garden three times in the plays. There was an actual garden in Holborn celebrated for its roses and saffron crocuses which belonged to a Bishop of Ely and later to Lord Chancellor Hatton, remembered to this day in the districts of London named Saffron Hill and Hatton Garden.

There is another reference to the strawberry in the plays: "Have you not sometimes seen a handkerchief spotted with strawberries in your wife's hand?" asks the scheming Iago of Othello. Ellacombe explains that the Otelli del Moro were a noble Venetian folk who came originally from Morea and whose device was a mulberry, the growth of that country. Shakespeare thought fit to make Othello a Moor and the embroidered arms a strawberry. Ellacombe suggests that the derivation of the word is not from the habit of placing straw beneath the plant but from an obsolete past participle of the verb to strew. It occurs in the Bible: "gathering where thou hast not strawed" and in Shakespeare's *Venus and Adonis*: "the top o'erstrawed with sweets."

PLATE 19

here's **Rosemary**, that's for remembrance; pray
you love remember, and there is **Pansies**, that's for
thoughts.
There's **Fennel** for you, and **Columbines**; there's
Rue for you and here's some for me, we may
call it herb of grace o'Sundays.
There's a **Daisy**, I would give you some
Violets, but they wither'd all when my
Father died.

Hamlet.
Act 4th Scene 5th

SUMMER GRASS

The grass illustrated in plate 26 seems to be the ordinary meadow grass *Poa pratensis* but there are others similar including both the annual ones and those with the creeping stoloniferous roots. Grass grows so quickly when it does start in May that it certainly appears to grow mostly at night. Shakespeare is using grass in the quotation from *Henry V* as a simile of growth and he uses it again in the same play (iii. 3):

> Mowing like grass
> Your fresh-air virgins and your flowering infants.

And in a simile in *Titus Andronicus* (iv. 4) he vividly recalls the result of summer gales: "I hang the head as flowers with frost or grass beat down with storms."

Grass is mentioned frequently in the literal sense: "lush and lusty", "how green", "a grass-green turf", "grassy carpet of the plain" and "a mountain top where biting cold would never let grass grow". In front of the pavilions where festivities and dancing took place in the summer there was often a "grass-plot" where the grass was short, and in *Love's Labour's Lost* (v. 2) the King says they have measured many miles to tread a measure on the grass.

It was evidently the habit to find the state of the weather from a blade of grass; Salarino in *The Merchant of Venice* (i. 1) says:

> I should be still
> Plucking the grass to know where sits the wind.

Perhaps the most pleasing picture of summer grass comes again from *A Midsummer Night's Dream* (i. 1):

> When Phoebe doth behold
> Her silver visage in the watery glass,
> Decking with liquid pearl the bladed grass.

THISTLE *Onopordum acanthium*

Although in the quotation accompanying plate 27 Shakespeare describes the thistle as "rough", in the only other mention he has noticed the love of a bee for the thistle. In *A Midsummer Night's Dream* (iv. 1) Bottom asks "Mounsieur Cobweb . . . kill me a red-hipped humble bee on the top of a thistle and, good mounsieur bring me the honey-bag" without breaking it.

There are many species of thistles in this country being found not so much on barren ground as on good ground that is not properly cared for. A story is told of a blind man, choosing a piece of land, who said "Take me to a thistle." Tusser in his *October's Husbandry* wrote:

> If thistles so growing prove lustie and long
> It signifieth land to be hartie and strong.

The Scotch thistle is a beautiful biennial often grown in gardens, growing up to five feet with striking sculptured leaves covered with white cobwebby hairs, and a rich purple flower which was the badge of the Stuarts and is still the national emblem of Scotland.

Frances Perry in *Flowers of the World* explains how this honour was accorded. In the early days of Scottish history armies only marched during the day but the invading Danes, thinking to catch the enemy unawares, moved at night and barefoot so that they should not be heard. One warrior stepping on a particularly fine specimen of thistle cried out in pain, thus rousing the Scots who drove them off with great slaughter.

THYME *Thymus serpyllum*

Plate 10 shows a bunch of exceptionally sweet-smelling wild flowers with the well known lines from *A Midsummer Night's Dream* where Oberon describes to Puck the bank of wild thyme on which Titania often slept "lull'd in the flowers".

Shakespeare recalled many of his favourite flowers in this play which according to A.L. Rowse was probably written away from London in 1593–4 when the playwright was touring with the Lord Chamberlaine's company of actors, following two years of the plague in the city. In Sonnet xcviii he proposes writing a "summer's story" and one might assume he had refreshed his memory of all the legends of the countryside, the fairy lore and the characters of the rural folk for use in the play. Nearly fifty plants, nearly all wild flowers, are mentioned in *A Midsummer Night's Dream.*

Thyme is nearly always referred to as "wild" by the poets. In *Lycidas* Milton wrote of the "woods and desert caves, with wild thyme and gadding vine o'ergrown". Francis Bacon described "those flowers which perfume the air most delightfully . . . being trodden upon and crushed . . . burnet, wild thyme and water mint". Gerard tells of the creeping "wilde thyme" and a white one planted in his garden for its fragrance. It comes from the shores of the Mediterranean but must have been well naturalized by Shakespeare's time, and yet, curiously, it never seems to have had a local name and is still known by its Latin name (*serpyllum* describes its creeping habit). Honey was much valued in mediaeval times before the widespread use of sugar, and bees love this herb.

PLATE 20

here is a Willow grows ascaunt the brook,
That shows his hoar leaves in the glassy stream,
Therewith fantastic garlands did she make
Of Crow flowers, Nettles, Daisies & Long-purples

Hamlet.
Act 4th Scene 7th

VETCH *Vicia sativa*

The cultivated vetch (plate 2) is not indigenous but was probably introduced to England by the Romans as an easily grown fodder plant. It appears to be larger in flower than the small purple vetch and the climbing vetchling of the woods and hedges. Sainfoin and lucerne are others of this family which are grown for fodder.

VIOLET *Viola*

The violet is one of the flowers most frequently referred to by Shakespeare (plates 4, 10, 12, 16, 19), and it can be blue, pink or white with heart-shaped leaves and stolons, or creeping stems that root at intervals. He has described it as purple, blue and blue-veined, and "forward" (early) and yet when "past prime [they] die as fast as they see others grow".

Always valued for its beauty and fragrance, the violet was the emblem flower of ancient Athens, and derives its name from the Greek *ion* or *vion* which became the Latin *viola*. The flower has given us the name of a colour, one of the hues of the rainbow, which is hardly consistent with its epithet "modest". Perhaps this refers to the bend in the slender stem, as if it is weighed down by the spur-like shape of the lower petal – the "nodding violet" in *A Midsummer Night's Dream*. Shakespeare vividly describes the little warm breeze that comes in spring and seems to wake the early flowers, wafting the sweet scent of violets from the mossy bank.

As he notes in *Hamlet* the scent is elusive, "the perfume and suppliance of a minute, no more". Later investigations show that the principal ingredient of the scent, ionine, quickly fatiques the sense of smell so that it can no longer be perceived.

There were many varieties of violet in Shakespeare's day; Gerard describes many flowers under this name and includes milk-white and double blooms which make "nosgaies and poesies delightful to look at and pleasant to smell". He also mentions a sweetmeat of violets and sugar and to this day crystallized violets are used to decorate cakes and chocolates.

WHEAT *Triticum vulgare*

Wheat (plate 2), the staple cereal, is not indigenous to England nor even to Europe. It came from northern Asia and is the first sign of civilization. When the nomadic tribes decided to settle it was because they had to wait for the wheat to come to harvest. It had been with us centuries before the Romans came for the name does not come from the Latin but from an old English word meaning "white", probably to distinguish it from the darker grains of oats and rye. Caesar reported that he found it growing when he landed and that he could victual his camp from the crop. The story goes that when his soldiers were reaping the wheat in Kentish fields they were surrounded and successfully attacked by the British.

> He that will have a cake out of the wheat needs must tarry the grinding.
>
> *Troilus and Cressida* (i. 1)

> And again, sir, shall we sow the headland with wheat?
>
> *Henry IV Part 2* (v. 1)

WILLOW *Salix*

Willow trees (plate 20) or withies are native to Britain and are common in Warwickshire where they are often seen bordering a streamlet leading to the river or along the Avon itself. They are usually pollarded or cut back to the trunk to make a dense head of small branches. These hang over the water and as the undersides are silvery white it is easy to visualize the reflection in the clear stream which Shakespeare so vividly describes.

"The rank of osiers by the running stream" is mentioned in *As You Like It* (iv. 3). Osiers are the thin withy branches which are still used to wreathe into baskets or to make coracles, which are light enough to carry and have been made since very early times. According to Ellacombe baskets were exported to Italy when the Romans were stationed in Britain. In *Romeo and Juliet* (ii. 3) Friar Lawrence carries a basket which he calls a "willow cage" and plans to fill it with baleful weeds and precious juiced flowers. In other plays the willow seems to be a symbol of a forsaken lover, either male or female. Desdemona in *Othello* (iv. 3) sings sadly "Willow, willow" and "the wreath wear I, since my love did flee", and Benedick in *Much Ado About Nothing* (ii. 1) offered to take the lovesick Claudio to a willow tree in order to make him a garland.

In contrast to other plants of that time, in the sixteenth and seventeenth centuries the willow does not seem to have been valued for any medicinal purposes, but at a much later date salicylic acid was made from its bark and has a number of uses.

ith fairest flowers
Whilst summer lasts, and I live here, Fidele
I'll sweeten thy sad grave: thou shall not lack
The flower that's like thy face, pale **Primrose**, nor
The azured **Hare-bell**, like thy veins: no, nor
The leaf of **Eglantine**, whom not to slander,
Outsweeten'd not thy breath:
Yea, and furr'd **Moss** besides, when flowers are none,
To winter-ground thy corse.

Cymbeline.
Act 4th Scene 2nd

WOODBINE *see* Honeysuckle *and* Bindweed

YEW *Taxus baccata*

Yew (plate 30) is an evergreen which grows into a thick shapely tree preferably on chalk or limestone country. It was often planted in churchyards and is reputed to be associated with resurrection.

> My shroud of white, stuck all with yew
> Oh! prepare it.
> *Twelfth Night* (ii. 4)

In the churchyard scene of *Romeo and Juliet* (v. 3) Paris gives careful instructions to his page:

> Under yon yew trees lay thee all along,
> Holding thine ear close to the hollow ground;
> So shall no foot upon the churchyard tread . . .
> But thou shall hear it.

It is usually said that the yew trees were planted in churchyards because the wood was then convenient for making the long bows of the archers. Bow-and-arrow warfare has now been superseded but the long-lived trees are still there.

> The very headsmen learn to bend their bows
> Of double-fatal yew against thy state.
> *Richard II* (iii. 2)

"Double-fatal" can be explained. Not only does the yew provide deadly weapons when dead but the living leaves are very poisonous to both animal and man. Oddly, the red fleshy berries which look so noxious are almost, if not quite, harmless. This is vouched for by Gerard who also refutes the superstition that it is dangerous to sleep under the tree. "When I was yong and went to scoole, divers of my schoolfellows and myselfe did eat our fils of the berries of this tree and have slept under the shadow thereof . . . without any hurt at all, and that not at one time but many times."

ithin the infant rind of this Small flower
Poison hath residence and med'cine power;
For this being smelt, with that part cheers each part;
Being tasted slays all senses with the heart.

Romeo & Juliet,
Act 2nd Scene 3rd

AFTERWORD

At the closing stage of this book it is appropriate to mention the Victorian artist, a Miss Girand, who has not only painted many delightfully well grouped flowers but has included accurate details of their nature, not always obvious but when looked at closely for identification found to be authentic, such as an unusual colour, spots on the stems or the shapes of the leaves.

In choosing the quotations she has managed to include nearly all the flowers of Shakespeare leaving out of the 180 plants she mentions mainly the trees and fruits.

In addition to the trees painted there are references to ash, aspen and sycamore and also palm and cedar. Among the fruits not painted are apples, plums, cherries and also the imported fruits, dates, olives, oranges and apricots. Vines are frequently mentioned. Salads in Elizabethan times were elaborate and more popular than vegetables as we know them. So we find the potato is a luxury; carrots, turnips, onions are briefly mentioned while leeks were despised. In contrast the salad could have included lettuce, radish, almonds, walnuts, mushrooms, garlic, samphire, marigolds, strawberry leaves and the candied petals of roses, violets and other plants. Sugar had become reasonably cheap and had superseded honey for sweetening. In addition there are frequent allusions to culinary aids in the use of saffron, ginger, pepper, mustard, mace, raisins and carroways.

It is interesting to compare the three plays which have the greatest number of references to plants: *A Midsummer Night's Dream*, *The Tempest* and *The Winter's Tale*. *A Midsummer Night's Dream* was written early in Shakespeare's career and according to Rowse while on tour. It includes nearly all the wild flowers, herbs and trees easily recalled from his youth with perhaps only the lily and the rose from the cottage garden.

The Tempest, a late play, is sited on an island so it concentrates on nuts, fruits and their trees, with weeds and natural undergrowth. It is in the other late play, *The Winter's Tale*, that we find all the garden flowers, the pot herbs and the culinary ones, that Shakespeare would know well in his garden at New Place, Stratford.

I am much indebted to Canon H. N. Ellacombe, who wrote *The Plant Lore and Garden Craft of Shakespeare* in 1878 from Bitton Vicarage, Gloucestershire. His erudite knowledge and the painstaking care with which he has listed all the plants and quotations has given me the basis for these notes, and I have included in the following pages two extracts from his book: the Seasons of Shakespeare's plays, and the Index of Plays, showing how the plants are distributed throughout his works.

I have enjoyed travelling through my *Complete Works of William Shakespeare*, looking for flowers in company with Canon Ellacombe and many others, including of course Miss Girand who has captured so well the essence of the quotations.

O, mickle is the powerful grace that lies
In herbs, plants, stones and their true qualities.
Romeo and Juliet (ii. 2)

And this our life, exempt from public haunt,
Finds tongues in trees, books in the running brooks,
Sermons in stones, and good in everything.
As You Like It (ii. 1)

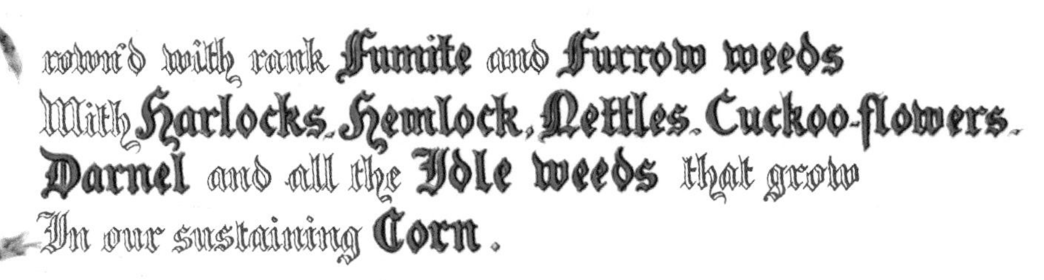

King Lear
Act 4th Scene 4th

THE SEASONS OF SHAKESPEARE'S PLAYS

Canon H. N. Ellacombe

In this paper I do not propose to make any exhaustive inquiry into the seasons of Shakespeare's plays, but (at Mr Furnivall's suggestion) I have tried to find out whether in any case the season that was in the poet's mind can be discovered by the flowers or fruits, or whether, where the season is otherwise indicated, the flowers and fruits are in accordance. In other words, my inquiry is simply confined to the argument, if any, that may be derived from the flowers and fruits, leaving out of the question all other indications of the seasons.

The first part of the inquiry is, what plants or flowers are mentioned in each play? They are as follows:

COMEDIES

Tempest. Apple, crab, wheat, rye, barley, vetches, oats, peas, briar, furze, gorse, thorns, broom, cedar, corn, cowslip, nettle, docks, mallow, filbert, heath, ling, grass, nut, ivy, lily, piony, lime, mushrooms, oak, acorn, pignuts, pine, reed, saffron, sedges, stover, vine.

Two Gentlemen of Verona. Lily, roses, sedges.

Merry Wives. Pippins, buttons (?), balm, bilberry, cabbage, carrot, elder, eringoes, figs, flax, hawthorn, oak, pear, plums, prunes, potatoes, pumpion, roses, turnips, walnut.

Twelfth Night. Apple, box, ebony, flax, nettle, olive, squash, peascod, codling, roses, violet, willow, yew.

Measure for Measure. Birch, burs, corn, garlick, medlar, oak, myrtle, peach, prunes, grapes, vine, violet.

Much Ado. Carduus benedictus, honeysuckle, woodbine, oak, orange, rose, sedges, willow.

Midsummer Night's Dream. Crab, apricots, beans, briar, red rose, broom, bur, cherry, corn, cowslip, dewberries, oxlip, violet, woodbine, eglantine, elm, ivy, figs, mulberries, garlick, onions, grass, hawthorn, nuts, hemp, honeysuckle, knot-grass, leek, lily, peas, peas-blossom, oak, acorn, oats, orange, love-in-idleness, primrose, musk-rose buds, musk-roses, rose, thistle, thorns, thyme, grapes, violet, wheat.

Love's Labour's Lost. Apple, pomewater, crab, cedar, lemon, cockle, mint, columbine, corn, daisies, lady-smocks, cuckoo-buds, ebony, elder, grass, lily, nutmeg, oak, osier, oats, peas, plantain, rose, sycamore, thorns, violets, wormwood.

Merchant of Venice. Apple, grass, pines, reed, wheat, willow.

As You Like It. Acorns, hawthorn, brambles, briar, bur, chestnut, cork, nuts, holly, medlar, moss, mustard, oak, olive, palm, peascod, rose, rush, rye, sugar, grape, osier.

All's Well. Briar, date, grass, nut, marjoram, herb of grace, onions, pear, pomegranate, roses, rush, saffron, grapes.

Taming of Shrew. Apple, crab, chestnut, cypress, hazel, oats, onion, love-in-idleness, mustard, parsley, roses, rush, sedges, walnut.

Winter's Tale. Briars, carnations, gillyflower, cork, oxlips, crown imperial, currants, daffodils, dates, saffron, flax, lilies, flower-de-luce, garlick, ivy, lavender, mints, savory, marjoram, marigold, nettle, oak, warden, squash, pines, prunes, primrose, damask-roses, rice, raisins, rosemary, rue, thorns, violets.

Comedy of Errors. Balsam, ivy, briar, moss, rush, nut, cherrystone, elm, vine, grass, saffron.

HISTORIES

King John. Plum, cherry, fig, lily, rose, violet, rush, thorns.

Richard II. Apricots, balm, bay, corn, grass, nettles, pines, rose, rue, thorns, violets, yew.

1st Henry IV. Apple-john, pease, beans, blackberries, camomile, fernseed, garlick, ginger, moss, nettle, oats, prunes, pomegranate, radish, raisins, reeds, rose, rush, sedges, speargrass, thorns.

2nd Henry IV. Aconite, apple-john, leathercoats, aspen, balm, carraways, corn, ebony, elm, fennel, fig, gooseberries, hemp, honeysuckle, mandrake, olive, peach, peascod, pippins, prunes, radish, rose, rush, wheat.

Henry V. Apple, balm, docks, elder, fig, flower-de-luce, grass, hemp, leek, nettle, fumitory, kecksies, burs, cowslips, burnet, clover, darnel, strawberry, thistles, vine, violet, hemlock.

1st Henry VI. Briar, white and red rose, corn, flower-de-luce, vine.

2nd Henry VI. Crab, cedar, corn, cypress, fig, flax, flower-de-luce, grass, hemp, laurel, mandrake, pine, plums, damsons, primrose, thorns.

3rd Henry VI. Balm, cedar, corn, hawthorn, oaks, olive, laurel, thorns.

Richard III. Balm, cedar, roses, strawberry, vines.

Henry VIII. Apple, crab, bays, palms, broom, cherry, cedar, corn, lily, vine.

ow dizzy 'tis, to cast one's eyes so low!
The crows and choughs that wing the midway air
Show scarce so gross as beetles: half way down
Hangs one that gathers **Samphire**; dreadful trade!

King Lear,
Act 4th Scene 6th

TRAGEDIES

Troilus and Cressida. Almond, balm, blackberry, burs, date, nut, laurels, lily, toadstool, nettle, oak, pine, plantain, potato, wheat.

Timon of Athens. Balm, balsam, oaks, briars, grass, medlar, moss, olive, palm, rose, grape.

Coriolanus. Crab, ash, briars, cedar, cockle, corn, cypress, garlick, mulberry, nettle, oak, orange, palm, rush, grape.

Macbeth. Balm, chestnut, corn, hemlock, insane root, lily, primrose, rhubarb, senna (cyme), yew.

Julius Caesar. Oak, palm.

Antony and Cleopatra. Balm, figs, flag, laurel, mandragora, myrtle, olive, onions, pine, reeds, rose, rue, rush, grapes, wheat, vine.

Cymbeline. Cedar, violet, cowslip, primrose, daisies, harebell, eglantine, elder, lily, marybuds, moss, oak, acorn, pine, reed, rushes, vine.

Titus Andronicus. Aspen, briars, cedar, honeystalks, corn, elder, grass, laurel, lily, moss, mistletoe, nettles, yew.

Pericles. Rosemary, bay, roses, cherry, corn, violets, marigolds, rose, thorns.

Romeo and Juliet. Bitter-sweeting, dates, hazel, mandrake, medlar, nuts, popering pear, pink, plantain, pomegranate, quince, roses, rosemary, rush, sycamore, thorn, willow, wormwood, yew.

King Lear. Apple, balm, burdock, cork, crab, fumiter, hemlock, harlock, nettles, cuckoo-flowers, darnel, flax, hawthorn, lily, marjoram, oaks, oats, peascod, rosemary, vines, wheat, samphire.

Hamlet. Fennel, columbine, crow-flower, nettles, daisies, long purples or dead-men's-fingers, flax, grass, hebenon, nut, palm, pansies, plum-tree, primrose, rose, rosemary, rue, herb of grace, thorns, violets, wheat, willow, wormwood.

Othello. Locusts, coloquintida, figs, nettles, lettuce, hyssop, thyme, poppy, mandragora, oak, rose, rue, rush, strawberries, sycamore, grapes, willow.

Two Noble Kinsmen. Apricot, bulrush, cedar, plane, cherry, corn, currant, daffodils, daisies, flax, lark's heels, marigolds, narcissus, nettles, oak, oxlips, plantain, reed, primrose, rose, thyme, rush.

This I believe to be a complete list of the flowers of Shakespeare arranged according to the plays, and they are mentioned in one of three ways – first, adjectively, as "flaxen was his pole," "hawthorn-brake," "barley-broth," "thou honeysuckle villain," "onion-eyed," "cowslip-cheeks," but the instances of this use by Shakespeare are not many; second, proverbially or comparatively, as "tremble like aspen," "we grew together like to a double cherry seeming parted," "the stinking elder, grief," "thou art an elm, my husband, I a vine," "not worth a gooseberry." There are numberless instances of this use of the names of flowers, fruits, and trees, but neither of these uses give an indication of the seasons; and in one or other of these ways they are used (and only in these ways) in the following plays: *Tempest, Two Gentlemen of Verona, Measure for Measure, Merchant of Venice, As You Like It, Taming of the Shrew, Comedy of Errors, Macbeth, King John, 1st Henry IV, 2nd Henry VI, 3rd Henry VI, Henry VIII, Troilus and Cressida, Coriolanus, Julius Caesar, Pericles, Othello.* These therefore may be dismissed at once. There remain the following plays in which indications of the seasons intended either in the whole play or in the particular act may be traced. In some cases the traces are exceedingly slight (almost none at all); in others they are so strongly marked that there is little doubt that Shakespeare used them of set purpose and carefully: *Merry Wives, Twelfth Night, Much Ado, Midsummer Night's Dream, Love's Labour's Lost, As You Like It, All's Well, Winter's Tale, Richard II, 2nd Henry IV, Henry V, 1st Henry VI, Richard III, Timon of Athens, Antony and Cleopatra, Cymbeline, Titus Andronicus, Romeo and Juliet, King Lear, Hamlet,* and *Two Noble Kinsmen.*

Merry Wives. Herne's oak gives the season intended –

> "Herne the hunter,
> Sometime a keeper here in Windsor forest,
> Doth *all the winter time* at still midnight
> Walk round about an oak with ragged horns."

If Shakespeare really meant to place the scene in midwinter, there may be a fitness in Mrs Quickly's looking forward to "a posset at night, at the latter end of a seacoal fire," for it was a "raw rheumatick day" (act iii, sc. 1), in Pistol's –

> "Take heed, ere summer comes, or cuckoo birds
> do sing,"

in Ford's "birding" and "hawking," and in the concluding words –

> "Let us every one go home,
> And laugh this sport o'er by a country fire"
> (act v, sc. 5);

but it is not in accordance with the literature of the day to have fairies dancing at midnight in the depth of winter.

Twelfth Night. We know that the whole of this play occupies but a few days, and is chiefly "matter for a May morning." This gives emphasis to Olivia's oath, "By the roses of the Spring . . . I love thee so (act ii, sc. 4).

Much Ado. The season must be summer. There is the sitting out of doors in the "still evening, hushed on

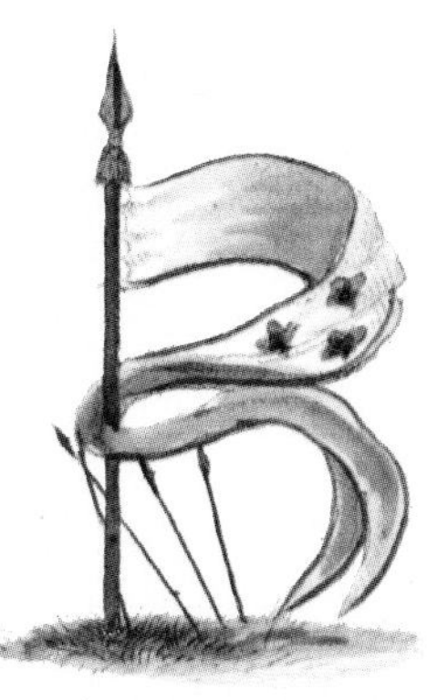

ut thou art fair; and at thy birth dear boy!
Nature and fortune join'd to make thee great:
Of nature's gifts thou may'st with **Lilies** boast,
And with the half-blown **Rose**.

King John,
Act. 4th Scene 2nd

purpose to grace harmony;" and it is the time of year for the full leafage when Beatrice might

> "Steal into the pleached bower,
> Where honeysuckles, ripen'd by the sun,
> Forbid the sun to enter" (act iii, sc. 1).

Midsummer Night's Dream. The name marks the season, and there is a profusion of flowers to mark it too. It may seem strange to us to have "Apricocks" at the end of June, but in speaking of the seasons of Shakespeare and others it should be remembered that their days were twelve days later than ours of the same names; and if to this is added the variation of a fortnight or three weeks, which may occur in any season in the ripening of a fruit, "apricocks" might well be sometimes gathered on their Midsummer day. But I do not think even this elasticity will allow for the ripening of mulberries and purple grapes at that time, and scarcely of figs. The scene, however, being laid in Athens and in fairyland, must not be too minutely criticized in this respect. But with the English plants the time is more accurately observed. There is the "*green* corn;" the "dewberries," which in a forward season may be gathered early in July; the "lush woodbine" in the fulness of its lushness at that time; the pansies, or "love-in-idleness," which (says Gerard) "flower not onely in the spring, but for the most part all sommer thorowe, even until autumne;" the "sweet musk-roses and the eglantine," also in flower then, though the musk-roses, being rather late bloomers, would show more of the "musk-rose buds" in which Titania bid the elves "kill cankers" than of the full-blown flower; while the thistle would be exactly in the state for "Mounsieur Cobweb" to "kill a good red-hipped humble bee on the top of it" to "bring the honey-bag" to Bottom. Besides these there are the flowers on the "bank where the wild thyme blows; where oxlips and the nodding violet grows," and I think the distinction worth noting between the "*blowing*" of the wild thyme, which would then be at its fullest, and the "*growing*" of the oxlips and the violet, which had passed their time of blowing, but the living plants continued "growing."[1]

Love's Labour's Lost. The general tone of the play points to the full summer, the very time when we should expect to find Boyet thinking "to close his eyes some half an hour under the cool shade of a sycamore" (act v, sc. 2).

All's Well that Ends Well. There is a pleasant note of the season in –

> "The time will bring on summer,
> When briars will have leaves as well as thorns,
> And be as sweet as sharp" (act iv, sc. 4);

but probably that is only a proverbial expression of hopefulness, and cannot be pushed further.

Winter's Tale. There seems some little confusion in the season of the fourth act – the feast for the sheep-shearing, which is in the very beginning of summer – yet Perdita dates the season as "the year growing ancient" –

> "Nor yet on summer's death, nor on the birth
> Of trembling winter" –

and gives Camillo the "flowers of middle summer." The flowers named are all summer flowers; carnations or gilliflowers, lavender, mints, savory, marjoram and marigold.

Richard II. There are several marked and well-known dates in this play, but they are not much marked by the flowers. The intended combat was on St. Lambert's day (17th Sept.), but there is no allusion to autumn flowers. In act iii, sc. 3, which we know must be placed in August, there is, besides the mention of the summer dust, King Richard's sad strain –

> "Our sighs, and they (tears) shall lodge the summer corn,"

and in the same act we have the gardener's orders to trim the rank summer growth of the "dangling apricocks," while in the last act, which must be some months later, we have the Duke of York speaking of "this new spring of time," and the Duchess asking –

> "Who are the violets now
> That strew the green lap of the new-coming spring?"

and though in both cases the words may be used proverbially, yet it seems also probable that they may have been suggested by the time of year.

2nd Henry IV. There is one flower-note in act ii, sc. 4, where the Hostess says to Falstaff, "Fare thee well! I have known thee these twenty-five years come peascod time," of which it can only be said that it must have been spoken at some other time than the summer.

Henry V. The exact season of act v, sc. 1, is fixed by St. David's day (March 1) and the leek.

1st Henry VI. The scene in the Temple gardens (act ii, sc. 4), where all turned on the colour of the roses, must have been at the season when the roses were in full bloom, say June.

Richard III. Here too the season of act ii, sc. 4, is fixed by the ripe strawberries brought by the Bishop of Ely to Richard. The exact date is known to be June 13, 1483.

Timon of Athens. An approximate season for act iv, sc. 3, might be guessed from the medlar offered by Apemantus to Timon. Our medlars are ripe in November.

Antony and Cleopatra. The figs and fig-leaves brought to Cleopatra give a slight indication of the season of act v.[2]

PLATE 26

he **Strawberry** grows underneath the **Nettle**,
And wholesome berries thrive and ripen best
Neighbour'd by fruit of baser quality;
And so the prince obscur'd his contemplation,
Under the veil of wildness; which no doubt,
Grew like the **Summer-grass**, fastest by night
Unseen, yet crescive in his faculty.

King Henry, Vth.
Act 1st Scene 1st

Cymbeline. Here there is a more distinct plant-note of the season of act i, sc. 3. The queen and her ladies, "whiles yet the dew's on ground, gather flowers," which at the end of the scene we are told are violets, cowslips, and primroses, the flowers of the spring. In the fourth act Lucius gives orders to "find out the prettiest daisied plot we can," to make a grave for Cloten; but daisies are too long in flower to let us attempt to fix a date by them.

Hamlet. In this play the season intended is very distinctly marked by the flowers. The first act must certainly be some time in the winter, though it may be the end of winter or early spring – "The air bites shrewdly, it is very cold." Then comes an interval of two months or more, and Ophelia's madness must be placed in the early summer, i.e., in the end of May or the beginning of June; no other time will all the flowers mentioned fit, but for that time they are exact. The violets were "all withered;" but she could pick fennel and columbines, daisies and pansies in abundance, while the evergreen rosemary and rue ("which we may call Herb of Grace on Sundays") would be always ready. It was the time of year when trees were in their full leafage, and so the "willow growing aslant the brook would show its hoar leaves in the glassy stream," while its "slivers," would help her in making "fantastic garlands" "of crow-flowers, nettles, daisies, and long purples," or "dead men's fingers," all of which she would then be able to pick in abundance in the meadows, but which in a few weeks would be all gone. Perhaps the time of year may have suggested to Laertes that pretty but sad address to his sister,

> "O Rose of May!
> Dear maid, kind sister, sweet Ophelia!"

Titus Andronicus. There is a plant-note in act ii, sc. 2 –

> "The trees, though summer, yet forlorn and lean,
> O'ercome with moss and baleful mistletoe."

Romeo and Juliet. A slight plant-note of the season may be detected in the nightly singing of the nightingale in the pomegranate tree in the third act.

King Lear. The plants named point to one season only, the spring. At no other time could the poor mad king have gone singing aloud,

> "Crowned with rank fumiter and furrow-weeds,
> With harlock, hemlocks, nettles, cuckoo-flowers,
> And darnel."

I think this would also be the time for gathering the fresh shoots of the samphire; but I do not know this for certain.[3]

Two Noble Kinsmen. Here the season is distinctly stated for us by the poet. The scene is laid in May, and the flowers named are all in accordance – daffodils, daisies, marigolds, oxlips, primrose, roses and thyme.

I cannot claim any great literary results from this inquiry into the seasons of Shakespeare as indicated by the flowers named; on the contrary, I must confess that the results are exceedingly small – I might almost say, none at all – still I do not regret the time and trouble that the inquiry has demanded of me. In every literary inquiry the value of the research is not to be measured by the visible results. It is something even to find out that there are no results, and so save trouble to future inquirers. But in this case the research has not been altogether in vain. Every addition, however small, to the critical study of our great Poet has its value; and to myself, as a student of the Natural History of Shakespeare, the inquiry has been a very pleasant one, because it has confirmed my previous opinion, that even in such common matters as the names of the most familiar every-day plants he does not write in a careless hap-hazard way, naming just the plant that comes uppermost in his thoughts, but that they are all named in the most careful and correct manner, exactly fitting into the scenes in which they are placed, and so giving to each passage a brightness and a reality which would be entirely wanting if the plants were set down in the ignorance of guess-work. Shakespeare knew the plants well; and though his knowledge is never paraded, by its very thoroughness it cannot be hid.

[1] If "the rite of May" (act iv, sc. 1) is to be strictly limited to May Day, the title of a "*Midsummer* Night's Dream" does not apply. The difficulty can only be met by supposing the scene to be laid at any night in May, even in the last night, which would coincide with our 12th of June.

[2] "The Alexandrine figs are of the black kind having a white rift or Chamfre, and are surnamed Delicate . . . Certain figs, there be, which are both early and also lateward; . . . they are ripe first in harvest, and afterwards in time of vintage; . . . also some there be which beare thrice a year" (Pliny, *Nat. Hist.* b. xv, c. 19, P. Holland's translation, 1601).

[3] The objection to fixing the date of the play in spring is that Cordelia bids search to be made for Lear "in every acre of the high-grown field." If this can only refer to a field of corn at its full growth, there is a confusion of seasons. But if the larger meaning is given to "field," which it bears in "flowers of the field," "beasts of the field," the confusion is avoided. The words would then refer to the wild overgrowth of an open country.

he even mead, that erst brought sweetly forth
The freckled **Cowslip**, **Burnet** and green **Clover**,
Wanting the scythe, all uncorrected, rank,
Conceives by idleness; and nothing teems
But hateful **Docks**, rough **Thistles**, **Recksies**, **Burs**,
Losing both beauty and utility.

King Henry Vth
Act 5th Scene 2nd

INDEX OF PLAYS

SHOWING HOW THE PLANTS ARE DISTRIBUTED THROUGH THE DIFFERENT PLAYS

COMEDIES

Tempest

Act I., sc. 1. Furze, Heath, Ling, Nut.
sc. 2. Acorn, Ivy, Oak, Pine, Reed.
Act II., sc. 1. Apple, Corn, Docks, Grass, Mallows, Nettle.
sc. 2. Crab, Filbert, Pignuts.
Act IV., sc. 1. Barley, Barnacles, Brier, Broom, Furze, Gorse, Grass, Lime, Oats, Peas, Piony, Rye, Saffron, Sedge, Stover, Thorns, Vetches, Wheat.
Act V., sc. 1. Cedar, Cowslips, Lime, Mushrooms, Oak, Pine, Reed.

Two Gentlemen of Verona

Act I., sc. 2. Ginger.
Act II., sc. 3. Lily.
sc. 7. Sedge.
Act IV., sc. 4. Lily, Rose.

Merry Wives

Act I., sc. 1. Cabbage,Prunes.
sc. 2. Pippins.
sc. 3. Figs.
Act II., sc. 3. Elder.
Act III., sc. 1. Roses.
sc. 3. Hawthorn, Pumpion.
sc. 4. Turnips.
sc. 5. Pepper.
Act IV., sc. 1. Carrot.
sc. 2. Walnut
sc. 4. Oak.
sc. 5. Pear.
sc. 6. Oak.
Act V., sc. 1. Oak.
sc. 3. Oak.
sc. 5. Balm, Bilberry, Eringoes, Flax, Oak, Plums, Potatoes.

Twelfth Night

Act I., sc. 1. Violets.
sc. 3. Flax.
sc. 5. Apple, Codling, Olive, Peascod, Squash, Willow.
Act II., sc. 3. Ginger.
sc. 4. Roses.
sc. 5. Box, Nettle, Yew.
Act III., sc. 1. Roses.
Act IV., sc. 2. Ebony, Pepper.
Act V., sc. 1. Apple.

Measure for Measure

Act I., sc. 3. Birch.
Act II., sc. 1. Prunes, Grapes.
sc. 2. Myrtle, Oak, Violet.
sc. 3. Ginger.
Act III., sc. 2. Garlick.
Act IV., sc. 1. Corn.
sc. 3. Burs, Medlar, Peach.

Much Ado About Nothing

Dramatis Personae. Dogberry.
Act I., sc. 3. Rose.
Act II., sc. 1. Oak, Orange, Sedge, Willow.
Act III., sc. 1. Honeysuckle, Woodbine.
sc. 4. Carduus Benedictus, Holy Thistle.

Midsummer Night's Dream

Act I., sc. 1. Grass, Hawthorn, Musk Roses, Primrose, Rose, Wheat.
sc. 2. Orange.
Act II., sc. 1. Acorn, Beans, Brier, Corn, Cowslip, Crab, Eglantine, Love-in-idleness, Musk Rose, Oxlip, Thyme, Violet, Woodbine.
Act III., sc. 1. Acorn, Apricot, Brier, Dewberries, Figs, Grapes, Hawthorn, Hemp, Knot-grass, Lily, Mulberries, Orange, Rose, Thorns.
sc. 2. Acorn, Brier, Burs, Cherry, Thorns.
Act IV., sc. 1. Elm, Honeysuckle, Ivy, Nuts, Oats, Peas, Thistle, Woodbine.
sc. 2. Garlick, Onions.
Act V., sc. 1. Brier, Broom, Cowslip, Leek, Lily, Thorns.

Love's Labour's Lost

Act I., sc. 1. Corn, Ebony, Rose.
Act III., sc. 1. Plantain.
Act IV., sc. 2. Crab, Oak, Osier, Pomewater.
sc. 3. Cedar, Cockle, Corn, Rose, Thorns.
Act V., sc. 1. Ginger.
sc. 2. Columbine, Cloves, Crabs, Cuckoo-buds, Daisies, Grass, Lady-smocks, Lemon, Lily, Mint, Nutmeg, Oats, Peas, Rose, Sugar, Sycamore, Violets, Wormwood.

Merchant of Venice

Act I., sc. 1. Grass, Wheat.
sc. 3. Apple.
Act III., sc. 1. Ginger, Sugar.
sc. 4. Reed.
Act IV., sc. 1. Pine.
Act V., sc. 1. Willow.

As You Like It

Act I., sc. 2. Mustard.
sc. 3. Briers, Burs.
Act II., sc. 1. Oak.
sc. 4. Peascod.
sc. 7. Holly.
Act III., sc. 2. Brambles, Cork, Hawthorn, Medlar, Nut, Rose, Rush.
sc. 3. Sugar.
sc. 4. Chestnut, Nut.
sc. 5. Rush.
Act IV., sc. 3. Moss, Oak, Osier.
Act V., sc. 1. Grape.
sc. 3. Rye.

All's Well that Ends Well

Act I., sc. 1. Date, Pear.
sc. 3. Rose
Act II., sc. 1. Grapes.
sc. 2. Rush.
sc. 3. Pomegranate.
sc. 5. Nut.
Act IV., sc. 2. Roses.
sc. 4. Briers.
sc. 5. Grass, Herb of Grace, Marjoram, Saffron.
Act V., sc. 3. Onion.

his brawl to day
Grown to this faction, in the Temple garden,
Shall send between the Red-rose and the White
A thousand souls to death and deadly night

King Henry, 6th
Act 2nd Scene 4th

Taming of the Shrew

Induction — Onions, Rose, Sedge.
Act I., sc. 1. Apple, Love-in-idleness.
sc. 2. Chestnut.
Act II., sc. 1. Crab, Cypress, Hazel.
Act III., sc. 2. Oats.
Act IV., sc. 1. Rushes.
sc. 3. Apple, Mustard, Walnut.
sc. 4. Parsley.

Winter's Tale

Act I., sc. 2. Flax, Nettles, Squash, Thorns.
Act II., sc. 1. Pines.
sc. 3. Oak.
Act III., sc. 3. Cork.
Act IV., sc. 4. Brier, Carnations, Crown Imperial, Daffodils, Flower-de-luce, Garlick, Gillyflowers, Lavender, Lilies, Marigold, Marjoram, Mint, Oxlips, Primroses, Rosemary, Rue, Savory, Thorns, Violets.

Comedy of Errors

Act II., sc. 2. Ivy, Brier, Moss, Elm, Vine, Grass.
Act IV., sc. 1. Balsamum, Cherry, Rush, Nut.
sc. 4. Saffron.

HISTORIES

King John

Act I., sc. 1. Rose.
Act II., sc. 1. Cherry, Fig, Plum.
Act III., sc. 1. Lily, Rose.
Act IV., sc. 2. Lily, Violet.
sc. 3. Rush, Thorns.

Richard II

Act II., sc. 3. Sugar.
sc. 4. Bay.
Act III., sc. 2. Balm, Nettles, Pine, Yew.
sc. 3. Corn, Grass.
sc. 4. Apricots.
Act IV., sc. 1. Balm, Thorns.
Act V., sc. 1. Rose.
sc. 2. Violets.

1st Henry IV

Act I., sc. 3. Reeds, Rose, Sedge, Thorn.
Act II., sc. 1. Beans, Fern, Ginger, Oats, Peas.
sc. 3. Nettle.
sc. 4. Blackberries, Camomile, Pomegranate, Radish, Raisins, Speargrass, Sugar.
Act III., sc. 1. Garlick, Ginger, Moss, Rushes.
sc. 3. Apple-john, Prunes, Sugar.

2nd Henry IV

Act I., sc. 2. Gooseberries, Mandrake.
Act II., sc. 1. Hemp, Honeysuckle.
sc. 2. Peach.
sc. 4. Apple-john, Aspen, Elm, Fennel, Mustard, Peascod, Prunes, Rose.
Act III., sc. 2. Radish.
Act IV., sc. 1. Corn.
sc. 4. Aconitum, Olive.
sc. 5. Balm, Ebony.
Act V., sc. 1. Wheat.
sc. 2. Sugar.
sc. 3. Carraways, Fig, Leathercoats, Pippins.
sc. 5. Rushes.

Henry V.

Act I., sc. 1. Grass, Nettle, Strawberry.
Act III., Chorus. Hemp.
sc. 3. Barley.
sc. 6. Fig, Hemp.
sc. 7. Nutmeg, Ginger.
Act IV., sc. 1. Balm, Elder, Fig, Leek, Violet.
sc. 2. Grass.
sc. 7. Leek.
Act V., sc. 1. Leek.
sc. 2. Burnet, Burs, Clover, Cowslip, Darnel, Docks, Flower-de-luce, Fumitory, Hemlock, Kecksies, Thistles, Vines.

1st Henry VI.

Act I., sc. 1. Flower-de-luce.
Act II., sc. 4. Brier, Red and White Rose.
sc. 5. Vine.
Act III., sc. 2. Corn.
sc. 3. Sugar.
Act IV., sc. 1. Rose.

2nd Henry VI.

Act I., sc. 2. Corn.
Act II., sc. 1. Damsons, Plums.
sc. 3. Fig, Pine.
Act III., sc. 1. Thorns.
sc. 2. Corn, Crab, Cypress, Darnel, Grass, Mandrake, Primrose, Sugar.
Act IV., sc. 2. Grass.
sc. 7. Hemp.
sc. 10. Grass.
Act V., sc. 1. Cedar, Flower-de-luce.
sc. 2. Flax.

3rd Henry VI.

Act II., sc. 1. Oak.
sc. 5. Hawthorn.
Act III., sc. 1. Balm.
sc. 2. Thorns.
Act IV., sc. 6. Laurel, Olive.
sc. 8. Balm.
Act V., sc. 2. Cedar.
sc. 4. Thorns.
sc. 5. Thorns.
sc. 7. Corn.

Richard III.

Act I., sc. 2. Balm.
sc. 3. Cedar, Sugar.
Act III., sc. 1. Sugar.
sc. 4. Strawberries.
Act IV., sc. 3. Rose.
Act V., sc. 2. Vine.

Henry VIII.

Act III., sc. 1. Lily.
Act IV., sc. 2. Bays, Palms.
Act V., sc. 1. Cherry, Corn.
sc. 4. Apple, Crab, Broom.
sc. 5. Corn, Lily, Vine.

TRAGEDIES

Troilus and Cressida

Act I., sc. 1. Balm, Wheat.
sc. 2. Date, Nettle.
sc. 3. Laurel, Oak, Pine.
Act II., sc. 1. Nut, Toadstool.
Act III., sc. 2. Burs, Lily, Plantain (?).
Act V., sc. 2. Almond, Potato.
sc. 4. Blackberry.

heir lips were **Four Red Roses** on a stalk,
Which, in their summer beauty kissed each other.

King Richard 3rd.
Act 4th Scene 3rd

Timon of Athens

Act III., sc. 5. Balsam.
Act IV., sc. 3. Briers, Grape, Grass, Masts, Medlar, Moss, Oak, Rose, Sugar, Vines.
Act V., sc. 1. Palm.
sc. 4. Balm, Olive.

Coriolanus

Act I., sc. 1. Corn, Oak, Rush.
sc. 3. Oak.
sc. 10. Cypress.
Act II., sc. 1. Crabs, Nettle, Oak, Orange.
sc. 2. Oak.
sc. 3. Corn.
Act III., sc. 1. Cockle, Corn.
sc. 2. Mulberry.
sc. 3. Briers.
Act IV., sc. 5. Ash.
sc. 6. Garlick.
Act V., sc. 2. Oak.
sc. 3. Cedar, Oak, Palm.

Macbeth

Act I., sc. 1. Chestnuts, Insane Root.
Act II., sc. 2. Balm.
sc. 3. Primrose.
Act IV., sc. 1. Corn, Hemlock, Yew.
Act V., sc. 3. Lily, Rhubarb, Senna, or Cyme.

Julius Caesar

Act I., sc. 2. Palm.
sc. 3. Oak.

Antony and Cleopatra

Act I., sc. 2. Fig, Onion.
sc. 3. Laurel.
sc. 4. Flag.
sc. 5. Mandragora.
Act II., sc. 6. Wheat.
sc. 7. Grapes, Reeds, Vine.
Act III., sc. 3. Rose.
sc. 5. Rush.
sc. 12. Myrtle.
Act IV., sc. 2. Grace (Rue).
sc. 6. Olive.
sc. 12. Pine.
Act V., sc. 2. Balm, Figs.

Cymbeline

Act I., sc. 5. Cowslip, Primrose, Violet.
Act II., sc. 1. Cowslip.
sc. 2. Lily, Rushes.
sc. 3. Marybuds.
sc. 5. Acorn.
Act IV., sc. 2. Daisy, Eglantine, Elder, Harebell, Moss, Oak, Pine, Primrose, Reed, Vine.
Act V., sc. 4. Cedar.
sc. 5. Cedar.

Titus Andronicus

Act I., sc. 1. Laurel.
Act II., sc. 3. Corn, Elder, Mistletoe, Moss, Nettles, Yew.
sc. 4. Aspen, Briers, Lily.
Act IV., sc. 3. Cedar, Corn.
sc. 4. Grass, Honeystalks.

Pericles

Act I., sc. 4. Corn.
Act III., sc. 3. Corn.
Act IV., sc. 1. Marigold, Rose, Violet.
sc. 6. Bays, Rose, Rosemary, Thorn.
Act V., Chorus. Cherry, Rose.

Romeo and Juliet

Act I., sc. 1. Sycamore.
sc. 2. Plantain.
sc. 3. Wormwood.
sc. 4. Hazel, Rush, Thorn.
Act II., sc. 1. Medlar, Poperin Pear.
sc. 2. Rose.
sc. 3. Willow.
sc. 4. Bitter Sweet, Pink, Rosemary.
Act III., sc. 1. Nuts, Pepper.
sc. 5. Pomegranate.
Act IV., sc. 1. Rose.
sc. 3. Mandrake.
sc. 4. Date, Quince.
Act V., sc. 1. Rose.
sc. 3. Yew.

King Lear

Act I., sc. 1. Balm, Vine.
sc. 4. Peascod.
sc. 5. Crab.
Act II., sc. 2. Lily.
sc. 3. Rosemary.
Act III., sc. 2. Oak.
sc. 4. Hawthorn.
sc. 6. Corn.
sc. 7. Cork, Flax.
Act IV., sc. 4. Burdock, Corn, Cuckoo-flowers, Darnel, Fumiter, Harlocks, Hemlock, Nettles.
sc. 6. Marjoram, Samphire.
Act V., sc. 3. Oats.

Hamlet

Act I., sc. 3. Primrose, Thorn, Violet.
sc. 5. Hebenon or Hebona.
Act II., sc. 2. Nut, Plum.
Act III., sc. 1. Rose, Sugar.
sc. 2. Grass, Rose, Wormwood.
Act IV., sc. 5. Columbine, Daisy, Fennel, Flax, Grass, Herb of Grace, Rose, Rosemary, Rue, Violet.
sc. 7. Corn-flower, Daisy, Dead-men's-fingers, Long Purples, Nettles, Violet, Willow.
Act V., sc. 1. Violet.
sc. 2. Palm, Wheat.

Othello

Act I., sc. 3. Coloquintida, Hyssop, Lettuce, Locusts, Nettle, Thyme, Sugar.
Act II., sc. 1. Fig, Oak, Grapes.
Act III., sc. 3. Mandragora, Oak, Poppy, Strawberries.
Act IV., sc. 2. Rose.
sc. 3. Sycamore, Willow.
Act V., sc. 2. Rush, Willow.

Two Noble Kinsmen

Introductory Song. Daisies, Lark's-heels, Marigolds, Oxlips, Pinks, Primrose, Rose, Thyme.
Act I., sc. 1. Cherries, Currant, Wheat.
sc. 2. Plantain.
Act II., sc. 2. Apricot, Narcissus, Rose, Vine.
sc. 3. Corn.
sc. 6. Cedar, Plane.
Act III., sc. 1. Hawthorn.
Act IV., sc. 1. Bulrush, Daffodils, Mulberries, Reeds, Rushes, Willow.
sc. 2. Cherry, Damask Rose, Ivy, Oak.
Act V., sc. 1. Nettles, Roses.
sc. 3. Flax.

Venus and Adonis

Balm, 27.

S.P.Q.R

The trees, tho' summer, yet forlorn and lean,
O'ercome with **Moss** and baleful **Misletoe**.

....

But straight they told me, they would bind me here
Unto the body of a dismal **Yew**:
And leave me to this miserable death.

Titus Andronicus.
Act. 2nd Scene. 3rd

Brambles, 629.
Cedar, 856.
Cherries, 1103.
Ebony, 948.
Lily, 228, 361, 1053.
Mulberries, 1103.
Myrtle, 865.
Plum, 527.
Primrose, 151.
Rose, 3, 10, 574, 584, 935.
Vine, 601.
Violet, 125, 936.

Lucrece

Balm, 1466.
Cedar, 664.
Corn, 281.
Daisy, 393.
Grape, 215.
Lily, 71, 386, 477.
Marigold, 397.
Oak, 950.
Pine, 1167.
Reed, 1437.
Rose, 71, 257, 386, 477, 492.
Rush, 316.
Sugar, 893.
Vine, 215.
Wormwood, 893.

Sonnets

Apple, 93.
Balm, 107.
Lily, 94, 98, 99.
Marigold, 25.
Marjoram, 99.
Olive, 107.
Rose, 1, 35, 54, 67, 95, 98, 99, 109, 116, 130.
Violet, 12, 99.

A Lover's Complaint

Aloes, 39.

The Passionate Pilgrim

Lily, 89.
Myrtle, 143.
Oak, 5.
Osier, 5, 6.
Plum, 135.
Rose, 131.

ACKNOWLEDGEMENTS

The compiler has found the following books most helpful:

Allan, Mea, *The Tradescants* (Michael Joseph, London, 1964)
Bentham and Hooker, *Handbook of British Flora* (Lovell Reeve, 1904)
Brown, Ivor, *Shakespeare* (Collins, London, 1949)
Burgess, *English Wild Flowers* (Warne, London, 1878)
Coats, Alice M., *The Treasury of Flowers* (Phaidon, Oxford, 1975)
Dana, Mrs William Starr, *How to Know the Wild Flowers* (Dover, New York, 1963)
Ellacombe, Rev. Henry N., MA., *The Plant Lore and Garden Craft of Shakespeare* (W. Satchell and Co., London, 1878)
Fairbrother, Nan, *Men and Gardens* (Hogarth, London, 1956)
Fitch and Smith, *Illustrations of British Flora* (Lovell Reeve, 1905)
Garett and Browning, *The Naming of Wild Flowers* (Williams and Norgate, 1952)
Genders, Roy, *The Cottage Garden* (Pelham Books, London, 1969)
Gilmour, John and Waters, Max, *Wild Flowers* (Collins, Fontana, London, 1954)
Johns, C. A., *Flowers of the Field*, ed., Boulger (Sheldon Press, London, 1925)
Johnson, Thomas, *Gerard's Herball*, 1636, ed. Marcus Woodward (Spring Books, London, 1927)
Keble, Martin, W., *The Concise British Flora in Colour* (Michael Joseph and Ebury Press, 1965)
Perry, Frances, *Flowers of the World* (Hamlyn, London, 1972)
Pratt, Ann, *Wild Flowers* (S.P.C.K., London, 1857)
Rhode, Eleanour Sinclair, *Shakespeare's Wild Flowers* (Medici, London, 1935)
Rowse, A. L., *Shakespeare the Man* (Macmillan, London, 1973)
Stearn, William T., *A Gardener's Dictionary of Plant Names* (Cassell, London, 1971)